HORSES AND PONIES

Their Care and Management for Owners and Riders

M. E. Tait

ARCO PUBLISHING COMPANY, INC.
New York

Published 1977 by Arco Publishing Company, Inc.
219 Park Avenue South, New York, N.Y. 10003

Library of Congress Catalog Card Number 73–91685

ISBN 0 668 03438 6 (cloth)
ISBN 0 668 03439 4 (paper)

Printed in Great Britain

Contents

Introduction

Bringing in the harvest with farm horses

THE AGE OF THE WORK-HORSE has passed almost everywhere into the age of motor transport. With it has passed much of the knowledge of horsemastership gained from everyday experience, and with it, fortunately, much of the abuse and exploitation of horses. For horses and ponies it is now the age of pleasure and competitive riding, with a new generation of horse-owners and of people who ride hired animals. Some of these are enthusiasts who have reached the highest standards in both riding and horse management, but there are a great many people who do not realise that knowledge is needed before owning a pony, or who trust blindly in any riding establishment, without being able to distinguish a reliable one from one which ignores basic principles of horse care.

There are already many books about riding and about horse management, and there are centres where courses of instruction at different levels may be taken. The purpose of this book is to show how an understanding of the nature of horses and of the principles of horse care and of elementary riding makes all the difference to the confidence, enjoyment and well-being of owner, rider, horse and pony. It is intended to help people who own horses or ponies, or hope to, whether for themselves or for their children, and also to help people who ride hired horses, whether regularly or only occasionally.

Brumbies, the wild horses of Australia, are descended from horses brought by early settlers

Pony trekking in Scotland with strong, sure-footed Highland ponies

1 Handling

Horses and Ponies in the Wild

The best way to understand animals is to watch their natural behaviour in the wild, or at least living free. The true wild horse of Central Asia is now almost extinct, but there are horses which have reverted to the wild, such as the mustangs of the United States and Canada and the brumbies of Australia. Others in many countries live as if wild, apart from regular round-ups for identification and sale of young stock, notably the British mountain and moorland ponies known all over the world as children's riding ponies.

Watching these horses and ponies one can see that they are herd animals, living mainly on grass, with instincts and physical and mental powers which combine to preserve the life of the herd. Alertness, quick reflexes and speed in flight are their chief defences against natural dangers, such as wolves and pumas. Their sense of smell and their hearing (with independently movable ears), are acute, and their eyes are set to see all round the horizon, but not well designed for close focusing. Remarkable powers of memory enable them to find their way over huge distances, to learn to avoid poisonous plants and dangers such as bogs, and also for each one to know every member of the herd and his or her social position within it.

The herd instinct gives protection and confidence to the young and inexperienced, and to all in time of danger. The herd is led by an experienced mare, and where life is dangerous the herd stallion maintains a strict discipline, driving the mares and remaining behind to fight if necessary. Where external dangers are few, increase of numbers makes starvation the chief peril, and a study of New Forest ponies in Hampshire, England, shows how their social organisation and daily routine are adapted for survival where food is scarce. They are usually seen grazing in small family groups, and each group, regardless of ownership, belongs to a larger group and these groups to one of four herds, each with its own territory for grazing, water and shelter. The daily routine is regulated according to the season; in

7

summer they graze early and late, with a midday rest when flies are most troublesome; in winter they use all the daylight hours and more to try to get enough nourishment from the poor grazing, while they also need to seek shelter at night from winter storms. Harmony in the herd is maintained by a social system which gives each animal a defined order of precedence. Each foal learns from the start every detail of its home surroundings so that it can gallop with confidence, avoiding rocks or bogs, and it will notice instantly any strange object. In play the foals express their joy in life while developing their powers and skills.

Behaviour as Domestic Animals

The secret of success in handling horses and ponies is in making use of their natural qualities; strength, alertness, speed, endurance, memory, social instincts, sensitiveness and gentleness, while avoiding, compensating or at least making allowances for circumstances which go against their nature.

The first thing is to give your horse confidence, and remove the nervousness which is natural to him when deprived of the security of herd life, particularly if he is young. For this the company of another horse is the greatest help, and if not a horse then a donkey or even a goat. Failing animal company you will need to give him extra attention yourself. Remember that he will seek the company of other horses and will dislike being left behind or made to move away from them. Yet he may be hostile to a strange horse, since his social relationship with it has not been established, and so care is needed in introducing a new horse into a field or stable yard with other horses who look upon it as their territory. Another important need is for the regular routine which is natural to your horse, and it gives him a sense of security to feel sure that his food and water, grooming and exercise will be on time: he can tell the time as accurately as any clock.

Your horse's confidence is just as important to you as it is to him, since his natural instinct when startled is to shy and when seriously alarmed to bolt, and a horse which develops a habit of bolting is not safe to ride, while even shying can be dangerous. He may be nervous of dogs, from their resemblance to wolves, until you make him friendly with individual dogs. Being a creature of the open plains, he

8

is afraid of anything which moves overhead above his line of sight, so it is useful to make him familiar with such things as washing blowing on a line and a man on a ladder. Loud and sudden noises, shouting and banging alarm him as, for instance, the band at a showground until he is used to it. A high wind instinctively makes him nervous, since in the wild he relies much on his sense of hearing for safety.

Horses have other natural qualities which enable them to respond to training. This training leads to the highest degree of confidence and co-operation in police horse work and in dressage: at a more ordinary level it provides reliable horses and ponies for novices and children as well as for experienced riders. A horse's or pony's powers of memory make learning easy, if not confused by the trainer's impatience, and lessons once learned are never lost unless reversed by a rider's incompetence. Another quality valuable in training results from the herd instinct, which makes it natural for horses to respond to discipline, to be reassured by other horses and also to be gentle and friendly. No horse is naturally vicious, he is only made so by human abuse. Your horse will normally obey so long as he understands what you want. Sometimes he will resist through fear or uncertainty, which may take patience on your part to overcome, and the easiest way may be to get another horse to give him a lead, for instance over a hedge, into a horse-box or through water.

In making use of the wonderful qualities of your horse you should never forget that as a living creature proper care and consideration includes giving him a share in the joy of life. You can vary his diet with things he enjoys, such as sliced apples and carrots (cut lengthwise so that they do not stick in his throat), and if he is stabled you can let him have a run and a roll in a field sometimes. When schooling, let him have a good canter afterwards and then walk on a loose rein. He loves to hear you talk to him in gentle tones, and to have his neck stroked firmly, but do not tickle his sensitive skin or pat him roughly.

Training the Handler
Once the natural reactions of horses are understood, difficulties can be anticipated and so far as possible avoided. Thinking ahead is a first principle in handling horses. The second important principle is to train yourself in self-control. Always move gently and confidently,

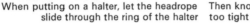
When putting on a halter, let the headrope slide through the ring of the halter | Then knot the headrope so that it cannot pull too tight

avoiding all quick and sudden movements and noise which are likely to startle him. Talk to him in gentle tones to soothe him, or to reward him for obedience, and in clear firm tones for command. Never shout or show anger, however annoying you may think him. Mutual confidence will then build up which will enable both of you to cope with unexpected difficulties. A strange horse knows at once if you have the right manner or if you are afraid of him and is likely to react accordingly.

Catching, Tying-up and Leading

Approach. In field or stable approach your horse quietly, but announcing your presence from a distance by voice. Walk up to his shoulder, taking care not to approach him from straight in front or directly behind, and pat his neck, not his nose. Then slip the halter rope round his neck by passing it first under and then over, close to the head. Put on the halter or headcollar, and release the rope from his neck to lead him away. In the stable he will move aside or turn to face you as you say, "Over", indicating with outstretched hand pointed towards his quarters which way he is to move. Then you can easily reach his head on the left (near) side.

Catching. If a horse or pony becomes difficult to catch in his field, avoid chasing after him, as this only increases his instinctive desire for freedom; a small pony will even sometimes make a game of not being caught. The presence of a second person may make him change his mind and give in, or you may slip the rope round his neck while he puts his nose in a bucket with a little grain, sliced apple or carrot in it. It may help to hide the halter from his sight while approaching, or even to catch him with a piece of thick string rolled up in the hand, and if he will let you get near enough you may catch him by first lifting up his near fore-leg. Remember always to move and speak gently, and let him feel your hand on his neck before slipping the rope round it. Never try to snatch or grab at him: his reactions are quicker than yours, and you will only make him afraid of being caught. It may be necessary to make him wear a leather headcollar all the time, but you must make sure it does not rub him. Never leave a rope halter on in the field, because it shrinks when wet.

The long-term cure for difficulty in catching is first to offer frequent titbits, from your hand if possible (otherwise left in a bucket for him), without attempting to catch him. After a while he will let you approach, and when you can stroke his neck while he eats, the time will soon come that he lets you catch him. Then lead him away, give him more food and release him. If you make a habit of catching him more often than when you want him for riding, and always have a titbit to offer, he will eventually become easy to catch.

Tying-up. Before grooming and saddling tie up your horse, either in his loose-box or outside, to a ring in the wall or to a fence. When a horse has to be tied up for any length of time in the stable, it is best to use a headrope which passes through a ring in the wall at about nose height to a block of wood on the floor. The purpose of this is to prevent the sort of sudden jerk which alarms a horse: if he pulls on the headrope it gives gradually. For tying-up without a wood block there are four important rules:

Always tie up by the headrope attached to a headcollar or halter, never by the reins.

Tie to something firm and strong, not less than 3 feet (1 metre) above the ground.

Have a length of about 3 feet (1 metre) of rope between the head and the post or ring: if you tie him short, say with only 18 inches ($\frac{1}{2}$ metre) of rope, he may jerk his head in panic, probably break the rope or the headcollar, and be difficult to keep tied up in future. If there is more than 3 feet (1 metre) of rope, he may catch his leg in it, which could make him panic, fall and injure himself.

Always tie with a quick release knot so as to be able to free him at once, with one quick pull, if in spite of all precautions he gets his foot over the rope. It is impossible to untie an ordinary knot with the weight of a horse pulling on it, and even a normally quiet horse or pony can be in trouble in a moment.

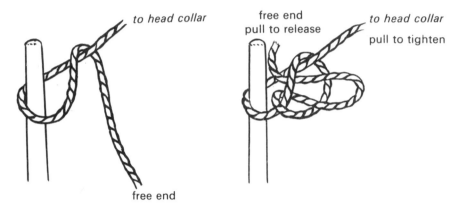

1. Make a loop round a post (or through a ring)

2. Make reverse loop back through first loop and pull tight

A quick-release knot is one which can be untied by pulling the free end of the headrope

Leading. To lead your horse out of the stable, hold the halter rope about 18 inches ($\frac{1}{2}$ metre) from his head in your right hand, with the long end of the rope held loosely in your left hand. Never wind the rope round either of your hands, and be sure that it can slip through them if necessary: you don't want to be pulled over or your arm wrenched if your horse is startled or prances. Steady him by voice, and walk ahead of him when going through the stable door; never let him push ahead of you. Glance back to see that he walks through quietly, without knocking himself on the door-post. Then walk level with his shoulder, with the rope slack unless you need to check his pace. Keep a gentle grip with the fingers of your right hand, so that the rope can be eased if he pulls suddenly. If he plays up, don't directly oppose his strength, which is so much greater than yours, or he may find he can get the better of you: you must manoeuvre him with give and take, if necessary circling him round you to keep control. If he stops, step back yourself, to remain level with his shoulder; encourage him to walk on by word and, if necessary a light tap with a stick on his flank where a rider's heel would be. Sometimes a hand slap on his quarters from someone else will make an unwilling horse move on. Never try to pull from in front of him: that only encourages him to resist, allows him to discover that he is stronger than you and, worst of all, it can teach him to rear up. Rearing, like bolting, makes a horse too dangerous to ride.

To lead a bridled horse, first pass the reins forward over his head.

For leading a ridden horse from the ground, attach the lead-rein to the underside of the nose-band. If there is no nose-band, and for leading a ridden horse from the saddle, an extra pair of reins should be used, or a single rein attached to a strap joining both rings of the snaffle.

Leading in a head collar

Saddling and Bridling

Saddle and Bridle. Each horse or pony should have his own saddle and bridle, so that you can ensure that they fit him well. The saddle must be the right width and length, so that it rests on the back only, not on the withers or loins: it must be wide enough not to pinch, and the padding must be so thick that the saddle does not touch the spine at any point. When you are in the saddle you should be able to put four fingers between the pommel of the saddle and the horse's withers, and anyone looking under the saddle along the spine should be able to see daylight. The padding tends to become flattened with age and will have to be re-stuffed from time to time so that an air channel along the spine is always maintained. The use of a saddle blanket is not a substitute for re-stuffing, and padding which is right for a horse in good condition may be inadequate for the same horse when in poor condition.

Girths should be smooth and supple, those made of nylon string and of folded leather being the most comfortable. The cheaper ones made of webbing are more likely to cause sores; they must be used in pairs, in case one breaks.

Stirrup irons should be wide enough to be sure that the rider's foot cannot become stuck in them, but not more than an inch wider than the foot. The stirrup leathers obviously must be of strong supple leather, and they are suspended from a metal bar with a safety-catch to release the stirrup in case of accident. Numnah (felt) saddles for small children riding Shetland ponies do not have the safety-catch, and so a safety stirrup iron is necessary. One type uses a loop of thick rubber for the outer part of the stirrup; another is like a half-shoe, closed at the front.

Saddling. The saddle is brought from the special peg where it is kept, with the irons run up the leathers to prevent them jangling when saddling and unsaddling. Lift the saddle above the horse's back, slightly forward of where it is to be, and draw it back to the lowest point of the back just behind the withers, smoothing the coat in the right direction: if ruffled the wrong way saddle sores could result. Check that the saddle rests properly on the back, not touching the withers or the spine, nor interfering with the movement of the shoulders. See that the girth on the right (off) side is not twisted, pull it

A pelham bridle fitted correctly, showing the loose throat-lash and the curb chain hanging in a curve

Bringing a general purpose saddle and a snaffle bridle from the tack room

through to the left (near) side and fasten the buckle, taking care not to wrinkle or pinch the skin anywhere. Let down the stirrup irons, and tighten the girth, gently and not too tightly: there should still be room for three of your fingers under it. Horses often blow themselves out to protect themselves against too tight girthing, so the girth must be checked a few minutes later. To make sure that the girth is not in a position to cause sores it is advisable, particularly with small ponies, to lift each fore-leg in turn, stretching it forward and upward. Roughness in girthing-up can make a horse jump away whenever anyone comes to do up the girth.

Bridling. To put on the bridle, first hang it on your hand to get it the right way round, then loop the reins over the horse's head just behind the ears, so as to have control of him while you remove the headcollar, or buckle the headcollar round his neck. Hold the top of the bridle in your right hand and ease it carefully over the horse's ears, while gently guiding the bit into his mouth with the left hand. Be careful not to catch the bit against his teeth, and if he is slow to open his mouth, put your left thumb into the corner of his mouth (where there are no teeth) and press on the bars (gums). It is most important to be patient and gentle: roughness can injure his teeth or mouth and make him difficult to bridle ever after.

Since it is his own bridle, already adjusted to fit him, the cheekstrap will be the right length to let the bit lie correctly just in the corners of the mouth: the brow band will not be tight, and the throat-lash long enough to be buckled loosely: the nose-band will not be tight or too low. The drop nose-band is worn lower than the ordinary one, and it is particularly important that it should not be so low as to affect the nostrils, nor so tight as to pinch in any way.

If you use a double bridle or a pelham bit the curb chain must lie smoothly and loosely in the chin groove. First hang the chain on to the hook on the right (off) side of the bit, then twist the chain round and round clockwise in your fingers until the links lie flat, and hang it on the left (near) side hook. You may hang the chain from the last link or a link two or three away from the end, choosing the one which makes the chain hang in a loose curve in the chin groove. To test for the right length, pull the curb rein gently, and see that the chain does not press into the chin groove until the cheek-piece of the bit reaches an angle of 45°. A curb chain fitted too tightly will cause pain to the horse and can even break his jaw.

Boxing

Most horses and ponies nowadays travel so often that they are easily led, by halter or headcollar, up the ramp into a horse-box. Boxing must be done quietly and carefully every time to avoid any sudden scare or slipping. If your horse is nervous or unwilling, do not hurry him. Another horse ahead giving him a lead usually brings success, or someone walking ahead of him with some carrots or a bucket of oats or horse-nuts. So long as they are quiet, helpers can encourage him from behind, pushing his quarters by hand or with a rope held from either side. Any shouting or bullying makes matters worse at the time and also, of course, for the future.

Each horse or pony should travel in a separate padded compartment, facing either forwards or backwards and secured by a headcollar or halter, never by a bridle. Makeshift vehicles without separate compartments or with horses standing sideways cause them great strain and stress in trying to keep their balance, and injury, often fatal, when they fall.

Driving Harness

This must of course be of the right size for the horse or pony, particularly the collar, which is not adjustable in any way. Its width must be such that it rests smoothly on the shoulders without pinching or rubbing, it must be long enough to be clear of both the withers and the windpipe and the lining and padding must be in good order.

To put on the collar, see that it is the right way round, then turn it upside-down to put it over the horse's head, turning it the right way up again before slipping it down the neck. To do this you had to untie the halter rope, so now tie it up again. Put the pad on the back just behind the withers and do up the girth, lay the crupper and breeching on the back, lift the tail carefully through the crupper and attach this to the pad. Remove the halter, unless you are going to leave it on under the bridle, put on the bridle and attach the reins after threading them through the terret rings. Now either back the horse into the shafts or pull the trap or cart up to him and fix the traces and the

Single driving harness

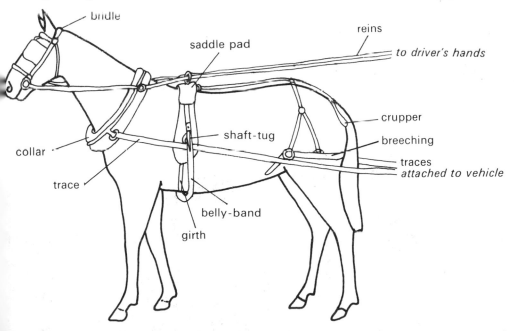

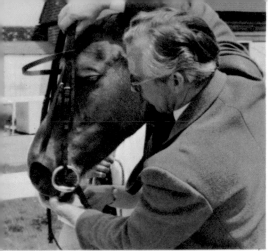

Putting on a snaffle bridle.

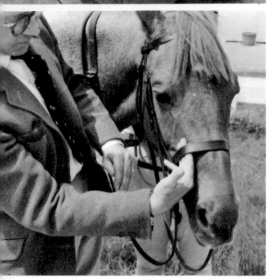

Placing the saddle.

Testing the nose-band.

Testing the girth.

Leading a pony carefully down the ramp from a horse-box.

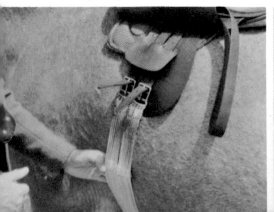

Single driving harness.

Shire horses in double harness.

breeching to it, and finally buckle the belly-band outside the shafts.

If you use a two-wheeled vehicle it is important to be sure that the balance is right, so that the shafts do not put weight on the horse's back, or lift him upwards by the belly-band. For this the shafts must be set on the vehicle to be roughly parallel with the ground when the horse is harnessed, and then the balance is maintained by adjusting the position of the people or other load being carried: the driver must be able to judge this by the feel. You should never use any fixed rein, such as the hame rein from bit to collar and the side rein, check rein or bearing rein from bit to saddle-pad. All of these can cause severe pain to the mouth and neck as well as strain when working.

Mood and Temperament

In everything you do with your horse, your own behaviour will affect his. If you are quiet, gentle and careful, carrying out each action in a way that he has been taught to expect, even a beginner can soon build up a relationship of confidence with a horse or pony, and this is to mutual advantage at any time and of great value in case of any sudden emergency. Any small fault in his behaviour will easily be checked at once by patience and firmness.

But if you are noisy, rough, careless or inconsistent in your ways, even the best-trained horse will become upset, and may soon take to bad habits which will make life difficult for both of you. He may even become so excitable that you cannot make him lead quietly in a halter or stand still when asked. Then you must quickly find the cause of the trouble to remedy it before it becomes a fixed habit. For instance, a pony bought from riding stables where he had daily hard work and constant companship of other horses may suffer from loneliness, boredom and lack of exercise. A mare in season or with a foal may be restless and difficult, as may a clipped horse in a cold wind. High winds, thunderstorms and rats in the stable upset most horses. If you cannot find any cause which you can remedy, or if you wait till the phase passes and you still cannot handle your horse or pony with confidence, it is best to change him for one of more placid temperament until you have more experience.

2 Learning to Ride

Choice of Riding School or Teacher

Anyone, of almost any age, with the right teaching, the right horse or pony and plenty of practice, can learn to ride. Patience in the early stages will be well rewarded, since a correct seat is the basis of all riding, elementary or advanced. Once you can maintain the correct positions at all paces, you will be secure in the saddle, in control of your horse and both of you will be comfortable. It is very much easier to learn properly from the start than to have to correct faults which have become a habit. Self-taught people who have "lived in the saddle" since childhood may find they have to start again at the beginning before they can achieve advanced horsemanship.

So unless you have a really expert parent or friend to teach you, it is best to find a good riding school, not necessarily the nearest and probably not the cheapest. There are first-class riding schools with qualified teachers: often they have an indoor school, useful at any time, and invaluable for winter evenings and bad weather. There are schools which specialise in teaching young children, usually suggesting they begin not younger than six years old, and there are schools which provide courses at all levels, including show-jumping and dressage. The schools to avoid are those where the teaching, if any, is worthless, because the teachers themselves lack knowledge and skill, and where the horses and ponies are badly trained and ill cared for.

With sound teaching and a choice of well-kept, well-trained animals to match your progress, you will make the best use of your lessons. An inferior establishment may seem inexpensive, but you can never learn to ride well with inadequate teaching and underfed, overworked animals, which may be too old, or much too young, and so little trained that they are unable to respond to the aids which you should be learning to apply. Advice on choice of a riding school can be obtained through your local Pony Club, or the Riding Schools Association. Your veterinarian and local SPCA (animal welfare society) may be able to help. In some places there are riding courses

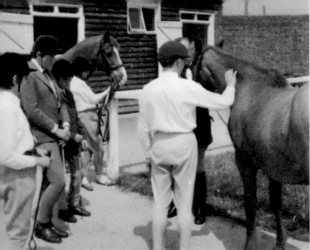

AT A RIDING SCHOOL

Approaching a horse.

Instruction in the stable yard.

Moving off.

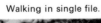

Walking in single file.

Cantering on grass.

MOUNTING

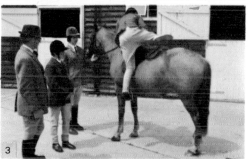

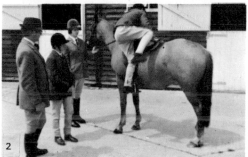

DISMOUNTING

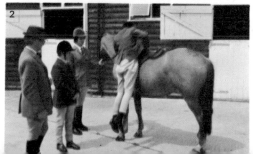

organised by the local authority, as for instance the Greater London Council. The Ponies of Britain Club provides information on trekking centres in Britain and Iceland. Some addresses are given on page 109.

Riding Clothes

As a beginner you do not need the expensive correct outfit of well-fitting jacket, breeches and leather riding boots. You will want jodhpurs to protect your legs from chafing by the stirrups and saddle (jeans are usually too thin), a plain shirt and a pullover or anorak for warmth: for heavy rain you need a strong riding macintosh, not a thin plastic raincoat which may frighten your horse when the wind catches it. Most important is a hard riding-hat, and strong shoes with enough heel not to slip too easily through the stirrup irons: jodhpur boots are good because they protect the ankles, and rubber riding-boots, but not ordinary gum-boots.

Mounting

You will be taught to mount with someone holding your horse's head, and also perhaps holding down the off (right) stirrup, so that in your first clumsy efforts your horse will stand still and you will not pull the saddle round. Take the reins in your left hand and grasp the withers with it, facing the horse's tail. With your right hand turn the back of the stirrup iron outwards, put your left foot in the stirrup and spring up from your right foot, turning as you spring, to reach the saddle facing forwards. With practice you will learn to spring lightly, pressing your left toe slightly downwards to avoid prodding your horse's flank as you turn, and to sink gently into the saddle, not jarring his back. A well-trained horse should stand still while being mounted, and by keeping control of the reins you prevent him moving forwards until you are ready. If he is inclined to move too soon, get off and remount again several times until he learns to stand still: if necessary you may stand him facing a wall or fence so that he cannot go forwards.

Now that you are in the saddle is the moment to check that it does not touch the horse's spine: if with your weight in it the saddle presses on the withers, you must refuse to ride with that saddle, however embarrassing that may be for you at perhaps your first riding lesson, and the addition of a saddle cloth does not solve the problem.

Dismounting

To dismount you hold the reins in your left hand, take both feet out of the stirrups, and with the hands on the pommel of the saddle vault to the ground, making sure that your right leg does not knock the pony's quarters. If the left foot is left in the stirrup until the right foot touches the ground and your pony is startled, you may lose your balance or even be dragged on the ground.

The Seat

It is worth your while to take a great deal of trouble to sit correctly from the start. Sit right in the middle of the saddle, leaving a hand's width of it behind you, and settle yourself well down into it, making contact with the thighs and knees. Your lower legs hang down to cover the girth, your heels slightly behind it, and the ball of your foot rests in the stirrup, your heels pressed well down. The toes point very slightly outwards, with the outer edge of the foot tilted slightly upwards. This position of legs and feet is the one which keeps you in the saddle: if the toes go down or the knees lose contact you will easily fall off. At first the position may feel strained, but if you concentrate on maintaining it, your muscles will adjust until it becomes easy and natural. You should sit straight up, but always with a supple back and your seat well under you, head up, shoulders square and elbows close to your sides. Fore-arms and hands follow a more or less straight line, palms facing inwards, fingers bent. The reins run from the bit to the hand under the little finger, or between the little finger and the next finger, passing up through the bent fingers to come out between forefinger and thumb. Fingers, wrists, elbows and shoulders must always be flexible in order to maintain a light contact with the bit as the horse's head moves with each stride as he walks. Your instructor may show you a number of exercises you can do from the saddle to make yourself more supple, but normally when riding it is important to sit still: fidgeting or rolling in the saddle is a sure way to give your horse saddle sores.

The Aids

When you ease the reins and press your lower legs back against his flank your horse will move forward. You will be taught to turn your

A good seat.

Below: A sequence showing the trot, riding on the right diagonal.

Above: Rider learning to jump, with neck-strap for holding on. Cavaletti make useful small fences for practising.

Right and below: The canter, leading with the right fore-leg.

well-trained horse by lightly pulling with the fingers of one hand while pressing with both legs, the opposite leg held further back: to slow or stop him by pressure from both legs and both hands, releasing the pressures as soon as he responds: to increase his pace by easing the reins and pressing with the lower legs, also exerting pressure from your back through the seat bones.

Naturally an untrained horse, or one dulled by constant bad riding, cannot respond to these aids, and that is why one sees riders with legs flapping and heels kicking, trying to get their horses to move faster. Riding like this you are only a "passenger", moving at clumsy paces of the horse's choosing, probably unbalanced and both of you uncomfortable. The true joy of riding comes from co-operation and understanding between horse and rider. When both of you have the same training you can develop his powers to the full, as he responds to your wishes in every detail. To achieve this takes time, with much patient practice, but you need never be bored, because there is always something more to strive for.

A good riding instructor will expect some proficiency at the walk before letting you trot, and may keep you sitting down (bumping) at the trot to improve your suppleness and balance before you learn the smoother way of rising at the trot. As one pair of the horse's legs touch the ground, say near fore and off hind, you rise, and sit down again on the other diagonal, as it is called. You should learn to recognise on which diagonal you are rising, because on a long ride you can ease your horse by sometimes changing from one to the other. When rising at the trot you will notice how important it is to keep the ball of your foot in the stirrup, so that your ankle is supple.

At the canter you will learn to adjust to the horse's movement, to sit down at the canter, that is not bouncing out of the saddle at each stride. Later you will learn to control with which leg he leads off, and how to change from one to the other. This is important when circling or turning, because for proper balance the inner fore-leg must lead: circling or turning to the left, "on the left rein", the left (near) fore-leg leads; circling or turning to the right, "on the right rein", the right (off) fore-leg leads. Leading with the wrong leg, called counter-cantering, can cause a fall: worse still is to go disunited, which means having changed legs with the fore-legs but not with the hind-legs.

With each increase in speed, you will lean slightly more forward, to maintain balance as the centre of gravity of your horse moves forward, until at a gallop you will be well forward, with your weight in the stirrups rather than in the saddle. It is natural for horses to love galloping, but a full gallop should not be allowed for more than short stretches and on soft ground: it is a great strain on the horse's heart, lungs and legs, and after all he was not designed to carry a rider. Many a pony has been ruined by children galloping wildly, and a proportion of young racehorses, too, although they are trained mainly at moderate paces. A very keen horse or pony, that is one which always wants to gallop ahead of other horses, must only have riders with the skill to control his speed without upsetting him. It is natural for horses to be excited by their speed, particularly when herd instincts are aroused in horses galloping together, and a normally obedient pony may "hot up", that is become difficult to hold, or keep control of his speed.

Jumping

When you are reasonably secure in the saddle and able to control your horse, no longer a passenger, is the time to begin jumping, at first on an experienced and willing pony over small fences about 18 inches ($\frac{1}{2}$ metre) high. You will be shown how to swing your body forward on taking off and straighten up on landing. The chief thing to avoid is getting "left behind" through not swinging forward enough or soon enough, and then you would hurt your horse's mouth with a jerk on the reins. So all beginners at jumping must make use of a neck-strap to hold on to, and both you and your horse will be glad of it. It is also important to keep the correct knee and leg position throughout the jump, or you may pitch forward over your horse's head on landing. You will learn to jump from a trot and from a canter, to control his speed so that he does not rush wildly at a fence, yet has the momentum to clear it. Later you will learn to judge the right moment to give the aid for take-off, and the length and number of his strides between fences. But do not tire or bore him with too long practice, and when out riding let him enjoy jumping natural obstacles, such as ditches, low hedges or fallen tree trunks. Never over-face him, that is ask him to jump anything which is not well within his powers at that moment. Over-facing is the surest way to make him unwilling to jump, and

Welsh Cob, 15 hands (1·50 m), can carry a heavy rider.

Shetland pony, 9 hands (0·90 m), for a very small child
or for driving.

English thoroughbred, 15·2 hands (1·55 m),
for speed and smooth action.

A big horse, 17·2 hands (1·80 m), can gallop and jump with a heavy rider.

Welsh Mountain Pony, 12 hands (12·20 m), an ideal child's pony for local shows, jumping and gymkhanas, with an adult's 15·2 hands (1·55 m) horse.

Two well-mannered ponies, reliable for beginners, 11·2 hands (1·15 m), for children, 14·1 hands (1·40 m) for teenage and adult riders.

when he stops suddenly you may fly over his head. Also, although artificial fences are designed to fall when knocked, in so doing his legs may be bruised, and it is best in every way to keep to fences which are not too difficult for him, and particularly because the fore-legs can become painful through jarring when landing from a height: momentarily all his weight and yours is on one fore-foot, which was not designed for carrying more than his own weight.

Schooling

Your horse was trained when young, and you have been learning, and now you need practice together in the movements necessary to give him balanced control of himself and you the skill to direct him. It is a good idea to spend a little time every day practising starting, stopping, backing and moving forward again in the various paces in so far as you have learned them. You can practise the walk, trot and canter, both collected and extended, in straight lines, keeping them really straight, in circles, making them true circles, in figures of eight and serpentines. You can make stationary turns, on the hocks (moving the fore-hand round) and on the fore-hand (moving the hindquarters round). Again you have no cause to be bored, because there will always be room for improvement, and the practice makes all your riding more enjoyable. Your horse on the other hand may well be bored, so do not keep him at it for long, and let him have a good run afterwards.

In learning to ride you need expert criticism all the time. You cannot see yourself (though some indoor schools do have mirrors), and even experienced riders have been horrified to see their faults shown up in cine films or photographs. Small faults can soon become habits and very difficult to cure.

Some patterns to ride when schooling

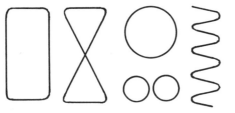

Let him have a good run afterwards

3 Hiring, Owning and Choosing

Hiring

After a course of lessons you will know if you really want to go on riding. Sometimes people thrilled by watching show-jumping on television find riding not so easy as the experts make it look, and then the idea no longer appeals to them; young children especially often lose interest when the novelty has worn off. So it is best not to buy a pony until you are sure.

You may have no intention of keeping a horse or pony, and hiring may well be the best way. People who live in cities may ride from country stables at the week-end, particularly if they have not the time or the money to ride often. You may be so ambitious to succeed in competitive riding that you want to do all your riding in a top-class school, training for show-jumping and dressage. Or you may want to ride just occasionally, on holiday, perhaps pony-trekking or trail-riding or just short rides for an hour or two. The more you have learned about riding and horse care the more you will enjoy this occasional riding. You may learn enough to be able to ride spirited horses unsuitable for novices, and you will not be persuaded by un scrupulous or incompetent establishments to ride unfit animals. You will have the knowledge to refuse the sort of undersized donkey or saddle-sore mule sometimes provided at tourist resorts in some countries, and you will know how to sit still and well forward in the saddle so as to avoid causing sores or over-tiring your hardworked mount.

Owning

If you are one of those horse lovers, young or old, who craves for a horse or pony of your own, there are three main obstacles to overcome. Can you provide suitable accommodation? Can you afford the cost of food, bedding, tack, shoeing and veterinary bills? Can you yourself afford the time to look after your horse, and find someone to stand in for you if you are away from home or ill? Or can you afford a groom and find a stand-in for him or her when off duty? If the pony is for your child, is he or she keen and responsible enough to attend to it before and after school, every day, always, or are you yourself willing and able to undertake the work and responsibility? If not, is there someone you can call on as substitute if your child is ill or away from home?

You may be lucky enough to live on a farm where there are other animals needing daily care, or near to a farmer willing to let grazing and take care of the pony if you are not able to. Or you may be able to afford the cost of keeping your horse at livery (boarding) stables. These may have fields where the horses can graze by day, taking natural exercise, but if the horses are stabled all the time, you will have to ride daily or arrange for someone else to exercise your horse. Chapters 4 and 5 describe the accommodation and daily care necessary for keeping your horse at home, whether stabled or living out.

Choosing

Before looking at any horses or ponies, or even at advertisements which may make you set your heart on an unsuitable animal, consider:

Who is to ride the horse or pony? One child, or several children of varying ages and experience? Or the whole family, including one or both parents? Or is it an adult: young, middle-aged or elderly, light or heavy, short or tall, beginner or average rider? (A really expert, experienced rider knows how to choose, within his means, the horse he wants.) No two animals are exactly the same, and there are horses and ponies to suit every type of rider—and some to suit none—and of course expense is usually a limiting factor.

Size. Obviously the horse or pony must be of a reasonable height (measured in hands of 4 in. (10 cm) at the withers) and of shape too. Neither a small child perched on a broad back with his feet half-way down the saddle flaps nor an adult with his feet near the ground can have proper control. More important still is the animal's strength in relation to the rider's weight and the work required, and horses come in as many shapes and sizes as people do. Difficulties need arise only when one animal has to suit several riders. A young child needs a small and narrow pony of about 11 hands, which will not be very strong, and as children often grow fast in height and weight such a small and lightly built pony may soon be outgrown. A tall adult needs a horse not less than 15 hands, and a heavy adult a big horse of 16 or 17 hands, or a weight-carrying cob. (10 hands equals 1 metre.)

Britain is fortunate in having nine native pony breeds, which are becoming popular all over the world for their excellence as children's and family riding ponies, being strong, agile, sure-footed, friendly and intelligent. They range in size from the well-known Shetland of only 9 or 10 hands—which is best kept as a pet or for driving, since its back is too broad to be really suitable for young children—through Dartmoor, Welsh Mountain and Welsh in the 11 to 12 hands range, Exmoor up to 13 hands, and New Forest, Fell, Dale and Highland from 13 to 14·2 hands including the Connemara from Eire. These larger breeds provide ponies suitable for teenage children and some of them are suitable also for adults. But do not be misled by false claims sometimes made for Dartmoor, Exmoor and Welsh ponies that they can carry an adult all day, an abuse sometimes suffered by ponies at the less reputable trekking centres. Of course a horse's weight carrying powers depend not only on height and build but also on age and condition, and this is discussed in Chapter 7.

Purpose. Your choice will depend on what sort of riding you want to do. Is it to be just quiet hacking, going for rides in the countryside or park? For this you need an animal of riding type, which means that he has a good sloping shoulder with well set-on neck and head, not too long a back and straight legs with sloping pasterns, so that he can move smoothly and without a tendency to stumble. He need not necessarily have great speed or elegance, though the more good qualities he has, the more enjoyable your riding can be.

Or do you aspire to serious competitive riding? If you are so experienced and skilled as to be ready to compete in the big national and international competitions, you will know how to choose a potential winner, but if you are not so skilled it is a mistake to think that by paying a high price for an already successful show pony or jumper a novice rider can be sure of winning: many a fine pony has been sold to such a rider and never been among the winners again. Top-class horses and ponies are almost certain to be specialists. They may have the perfect conformation and paces for showing, exceptional jumping ability, or the speed, balance and handiness needed for gymkhanas and polo. For the ordinary rider it is possible to find an animal which combines in some degree two or more of these qualities, and then it is up to you to develop his full potential. For instance, a reasonably good-looking pony may win a small show class if you have trained him to move as well as he can: he may not have great jumping ability, but trained to be reliable he may often win over potentially better jumpers which make careless mistakes or sometimes stop or run out at a fence. With training and practice any pony can attain a measure of success in gymkhanas unless he is particularly slow.

Temperament. Perhaps the most important thing to look for in the horse or pony you buy is the right temperament. For a novice rider this means a good-tempered, placid animal, well-trained and willing. These qualities are essential, and to find them you may have to pay more than you expected, or else put up with fewer good looks than you had hoped for. So often horses or ponies which are placid enough to be controlled by an inexperienced rider, and not to unseat him or her by sudden shying or dashing off at a gallop, are sluggish or even obstinate. An adult who needs a quiet horse because he is nervous or elderly might put up with sluggishness, but that is not a good thing for a child who is learning to ride. It is impossible to learn how to use the aids with a pony who will not respond. Again, a pony may be so gentle and friendly that a small child is safe with it as a pet, but which when ridden may be too excitable or too wilful for the child to control it. It is said that the perfect beginner's pony is worth its weight in gold, and certainly it can be difficult to find: so often it is passed on within a family or to friends without ever being offered for sale.

It is usually best for a novice rider to buy a horse or pony not less than nine or ten years old, even as much as from fifteen to twenty years old for a very young child or an elderly adult. A young animal cannot be relied upon not to take fright suddenly, and being deprived of the reassurance which the company of older horses would give him, he needs to take his confidence from a skilled rider. His education should continue for several years after his first training, and an inexperienced rider cannot give either training or confidence. Young horses and ponies are just as quick to learn bad habits as good ones.

If from high spirits he begins to buck and you fall off: or if something frightens him and you cannot prevent him from swinging round and dashing for home, then he may take to bucking every time you ride him or running away at the slightest alarm. An experienced rider would have stopped him bucking by sitting firmly and keeping his head up until he learned to control that impulse, and would have held him steady to calm his sudden fears. He becomes accustomed to behave well, and if of a naturally quiet temperament will in a few years be ideal for a novice rider. Others are naturally so highly strung that they will always need an experienced rider.

As the novice rider becomes more competent, he will learn to control behaviour which previously was too much for him, and experienced riders prefer a horse which moves gaily and can gallop, even if it is a bit excitable. But at each stage it is most important that the rider should not be over-horsed. This means not just too big a horse, but one he cannot properly control, and he is likely to develop bad riding habits, such as pulling heavily on the reins. For the horse, what started as nervousness or high spirits may turn into dangerous habits such as rearing or bolting, or at least such annoying habits as prancing about and jogging instead of walking.

When two or three children share one pony it must be quiet enough for the least experienced, and if a rider, young or old, has become nervous through trying to ride a horse he could not control or because of an accident, confidence can be restored by riding a very quiet animal for a while.

Soundness. It is unwise to buy a horse or pony without a certificate of soundness from a veterinarian, who has just examined it for soundness as described in Chapter 7. Obviously it is important to be sure that there is no disease or injury likely to cause permanent disability and it can be dangerous to ride a horse which suffers from heart trouble or partial blindness. Soundness of wind, that is absence of lung or bronchial trouble, is important for active riding, though a slight defect may be tolerable, on veterinary advice, for quiet hacking only. The veterinarian will also be able to judge the horse's age, accurately up to 8 years old, approximately after that.

Finding your Horse or Pony

It may be true that the perfect horse is so rare as to be beyond the means of most people, but many an owner believes his own horse or pony to be perfect, and it is worth taking a lot of trouble to find the right one. You may know of him already, if he is for sale by a friend or a local riding school or dealer. Or you may hear of him through an advertisement, either in a local paper or a riding or farming magazine, and then you may have to go and see many animals before finding a suitable one. Probably the best method is through the recommendation of a friend who understands both horses and your own capabilities. In this way advice through the local branch of the Pony Club can be most helpful, since their officials and instructors are likely to have personal knowledge of local ponies and their riders through seeing them at rallies and camps. Only very experienced horsemen should buy at auction: any unknown horse, even though warranted sound and free from vice may appear to be quiet and well-mannered through lack of condition, and later with proper feeding become unmanageable by a novice.

Before deciding to buy, the prospective rider should try the horse or pony thoroughly, to see if he goes as well for him or her as for the owner or for the dealer's skilled rider. Sometimes it is possible to have a pony on trial for a few days or a week, to give time for him to settle down and see if he is really right for you. You cannot expect this from an owner, because if you do not ride well you could do harm to his training in that time. A local riding school may well be willing to make an exchange if the pony you have chosen becomes too much for you, without the hard work and the companionship of many horses which he was accustomed to. If in spite of all care and good advice from knowledgeable friends you find you have made a mistake, it is only fair to yourself, or your child, and the pony to try again. Of course you will lose the difference between the buying and selling prices, but that is a small matter compared with the advantage of being really happy with your pony, or confident that your child can manage him.

4 Stable Management

MOST PRIVATELY KEPT PONIES and many horses too live mainly out at grass, but knowledge of stable management is necessary for all owners for two reasons. One is that the general principles of stable care apply to all horses, in or out, and the second is that even those which normally live out must be stabled at times. Your horse must be brought in if ill or injured and in severe weather. He may be stabled for a period of training for some competition so as to control his feeding and exercise, or perhaps just overnight before a gymkhana day, so that he is not blown out with grass and to keep him clean and dry in wet weather. If you intend to keep your horse permanently stabled it is important also for you to know what it will cost you for food and bedding, and how much work is involved in daily care, including exercise: you cannot expect your horse to be healthy, let alone happy and well-behaved, if he spends most of his time standing in a stable with only week-end exercise.

Riding schools usually keep their animals stabled, and at the best of them you can learn good stable management. As described in Chapter 2, you need to find a reputable place which is willing to teach you. To become really expert you can join a residential course, leading to an examination under the British Horse Society.

The Stable

The best sort of stabling is a modern range of brick-built loose-boxes, light, roomy, well drained and well ventilated, with running water and electric light, even electric heating, with forage store and tack-room, all built round an enclosed stable yard. If you have old-fashioned stables, divided into stalls where the horses have to be tied, it is usually possible to convert the stalls to a smaller number of loose-boxes by alterations to the partitions. For a horse each loose-box should measure at least 12×10 feet ($3\frac{1}{2} \times 3$ metres), and for ponies naturally the dimensions can be less, say 10×8 feet ($3 \times 2\frac{1}{2}$ metres) for a 13-hand pony, down to 8×6 feet ($2\frac{1}{2} \times 2$ metres) for a small Shetland.

A home-built range of loose-boxes

Another range of timber loose-boxes

It is important for the roof to be high enough for the horse or pony: otherwise his head can be seriously injured when he throws it up suddenly through being startled. Lower down the scale comes really old stables, out-houses, barns or garages, needing a lot of alteration. They may be dark, damp and unventilated, so that you need to make windows, with louvred shutters for draught-free ventilation, and divided doors for the horses to look out of the top half. It should be possible to lay new concrete flooring, with drainage channels leading to a sump behind the stable. You may find that the building you hoped to convert is too small, too flimsy, or the roof too low and you decide to rebuild it. Hints on doing this are given in Chapter 5 in the section on field shelters. However, you may well prefer an easier and possibly better alternative, a prefabricated timber stable, to be put up by yourself or a handyman in the place most convenient to you and your horse. In Britain you will probably need planning permission. You can buy anything from a small stable for one animal to a range of loose-boxes with tack-room and forage store. A difficulty which can arise with timber stables for more than one horse is that sometimes a horse will express its rivalry with another by kicking the stable wall: in emergency and if the loose-box is large enough, the wall may be lined with straw bales.

Feeding

The natural food of horses is grass, and there is nothing more nourishing for them than the young grass of spring and early summer in temperate lands on good soil. The foals are born at this time, when the mare can convert the good grass into milk for them. By late summer the grass begins to lose its food value and in winter contains very little nourishment. Wild horses have to travel great distances to find enough to eat then, and the free-living moorland ponies whose grazing areas are restricted and on poor soils may be in very poor condition before spring returns.

The stabled horse lives mainly on hay, which should be made from the rich grass of early summer, dried quickly in good weather, not from the second growth of late summer. It may be greenish or yellow in colour and should have a pleasant sweet smell with the seeds still in the grass heads. It must never be pale grey or dark in colour, mouldy, dusty or rank-smelling, and such hay is not only worthless but harmful in that the mouldy dust can damage the horse's lungs, and yours too. Good hay is more nourishing than all except the best spring grass, and for a working horse it is better even than this. The high moisture content of grass blows out the horse in such a way that strenuous exercise would damage his wind, his breathing. One sometimes sees gypsy horses, fat from roadside grazing, distressed as they draw heavy caravans.

The wild horse takes some exercise while grazing and sometimes canters for the joy of it, and so he keeps fit enough to run from danger when necessary, but he would soon lose condition if he had to do a full day's work on grass alone. The working horse needs a daily ration of grain, usually of crushed oats and mixed with bran or chaff for digestibility. (Chaff should be chopped up good quality hay, but sometimes it is only straw.) The difficulty for inexperienced horse-keepers is that the amount of grain needed varies enormously according to the size of the animal and the amount of work he is doing. A child's small pony must not be given oats at all, because they can have an almost intoxicating effect, turning an otherwise quiet pony into an impossibly excitable one. Ponies from 12 to 14 hands (1·20 to 1·40 metres) being used for strenuous exercise may need from 2 to 8 pounds (1 to 4 kilograms) of grain daily and horses of 15 hands (1·50 metres) and over from 6 to 10 pounds (3 to 5 kilograms) daily. This concentrated food replaces hay to some extent, but a daily supply of hay (or chaff) is essential as roughage to aid digestion as well as for nourishment. Your horse should be offered as much hay as he will eat, anything from 10 to 25 pounds (6 to 13 kilograms) a day, depending on how much grain he is having. Hay racks should be set at muzzle height, not high up as they used to be, a bad custom causing dust and hayseeds to fall in the horse's eyes, ears and nostrils. Ponies are sometimes wasteful with their hay, trampling underfoot all but the flavours they like best, and this can be prevented to some extent by feeding from a hay-net. This should be tied to a ring fixed not less than 5 feet (1½ metres) high on the stable wall, secured high enough to avoid the risk of catching a foot in the net when it is empty and sags down. Never fix a nail in a stable anywhere: it could cost your pony his eye.

The hay-net is tied with a quick-release knot, not less than a metre above ground level

Horses do well to refuse musty hay which has been stored damp, grey hay which was caught by bad weather after cutting and lay in the rain till the goodness was washed out of it, hay containing thistles or, worse still, poisonous weeds. They do usually prefer clover hay, which can be too fattening, or mixture (part clover), sanfoin, lucerne, or good meadow hay, which contains various wild plants besides grass: they often dislike hay made from the grass crop of sown grass leys.

A convenient way of feeding concentrates nowadays is with cubes, nuts or pellets made from a mixture of grains and hay, the best of them made to a fixed formula with added minerals and vitamins. Some varieties claim to be sufficient without feeding any hay or grass for roughage, but this claim should not be relied upon. In any case you will need to give about twice the weight of cubes compared with grain, since they are partly made of hay.

Horses have a small stomach and a very long gut, which must be kept supplied by frequent feeds, as happens naturally in the wild or out at grass. They sleep for only a few hours at a time, grazing for long and short periods throughout the twenty-four hours, usually in a regular pattern. Therefore the stabled horse must be fed not less than four times a day, early in the morning, about noon, afternoon and evening and then left with a rack or net of hay for the night. If he is not doing much work, and so living mainly on hay, three feeds may be enough, the first a bit later and the last a bit earlier, since hay takes a long time to eat. The grain or horse-nuts must be divided into the four feeds in proportions according to the pattern of work, the lighter feeds before work and the heavier after. Always leave an hour for digestion after feeding. The grain or horse-nuts are given in the manger, cleaned out thoroughly each time, or in a clean bucket.

Living on dry food, your horse will appreciate juicy extras such as a little cut grass or clover in summer, and in winter a pound or two of sliced apples or carrots cut lengthwise: whole apples or chunks of carrot can cause choking. A brick of salt should be provided in a holder on the wall or a lump of rock salt in the manger.

New Forest ponies seeking clean water in the centre of a pond

Horses enjoying clean running water   Fetching water

Water

The stabled horse needs large amounts of water, and, as with his food, at intervals throughout the twenty-four hours. Therefore clean water should be available at all times in his box. If his bucket is empty before a feed, it is important to offer him water first, but the old belief that horses must never be allowed to drink other than before a feed dates from the bad old days when many horses were taken out to water only once or twice a day. No wonder they had to drink an enormous amount at one time, and if that should be after a feed of grain, colic could result. It is true that horses in the wild sometimes drink only once a day, but the grass they eat contains water which is released in digestion, and also it is often wet with rain or dew.

Horses are very particular about clean water, instinct teaching them to refuse tainted water however thirsty they may be. Therefore fresh water in a well-rinsed bucket should be offered before each feed, even if the bucket is still half full. Water from a tap or pump is usually best, though where the tap supply is heavily chlorinated horses do appreciate water from a clear-running stream. Never give stagnant water from a pond or ditch. Another old-fashioned idea is that a horse must not be allowed to drink when he comes in hot from work. It is now considered good for him to have half a bucket at once, and more later

45

when he has cooled down. In the same way, he can enjoy a short drink from a stream during a long ride, but do not let him drink for too long. In winter, when water may be scarcely above freezing, for a hot horse it should be "chilled". This very misleading term means the opposite —that the water should be warmed, with water from the hot tap, which you must fetch from the house, unless you have an electric point in the tack-room to heat it.

Bedding

Wheat straw is usually considered the best bedding, since it remains springy longer than oat straw, and barley straw must be avoided because of the irritating scratchy seed-heads in it. Some people prefer to use wood-chips or peat litter, which are good for making a thick absorbent layer, particularly for stables which lack drainage: they are useful also for horses which blow themselves out by eating straw, which of course, is not so nourishing as their proper food of hay and grain.

To prepare a loose-box, first scrub the floor with water and the stiff stable broom and see that the drains are clear. When the floor is dry, open a bale of straw and toss it all over the floor and then tease it with the pitch fork so that it lies in a criss-cross manner, to make a bed at least 6 inches (15 cm.) thick, which may well take more than one bale. Arrange extra straw along the walls, for the comfort of your horse when lying down, and to stop draughts.

First thing next morning remove the loose droppings, using a skep (basket) or a bucket kept for that purpose only. Then with fork and shovel remove the wet and dirty straw, piling the unsoiled straw along the walls, and leave the centre floor to dry, after brushing or washing it as necessary. Spread out the straw again for your horse to stand on and before each feed in the day, remove the droppings. In the evening arrange the bed for the night, adding fresh straw. It is no economy to skimp the depth of bed, since a shallow one becomes more quickly soiled. A warm and comfortable bed encourages your horse to sleep lying down, which gives him better rest than if he sleeps standing up. Also the bed should be made even and secure to stand on: you may have heard that a horse can be injured by being "cast" in the stable, which means that he slipped and fell. Finally it is important to make

Tools for grooming. *Back*: saddle soap, metal curry comb, neats'-foot oil, dandy brush. *Front*: water brush, rubber curry comb, body brush. An important tool not shown is the hoof pick.

the bed clean and dry every day and to keep the drainage clear. In a warm stable urine gives off ammonia, which irritates the eyes and nose, and standing in a dirty stable is likely to cause foot troubles such as thrush and cracked heels.

Use a wheelbarrow or a square piece of sacking to remove the soiled straw and droppings to make a pile well away from the stables. After making a neat heap as high as convenient, start another one beside it, and before this one gets too high the first will have rotted down for easy removal as fertiliser. In summer the pile in use should be sprayed daily with insecticide to control flies.

Grooming

The Coat. Grooming cleans and massages, and daily grooming is essential for the stabled horse, not just for appearance but for the health of his skin. Sweat and dirt which would clog the pores of the skin are cleaned out by the body brush. Start at the neck on the near side, using the left hand in a semicircular motion, working towards the hind quarters—repeat the process on the off side using the right hand: be careful with the underneath, which is inclined to be ticklish. After every few strokes with the brush, the dirt has to be scraped out

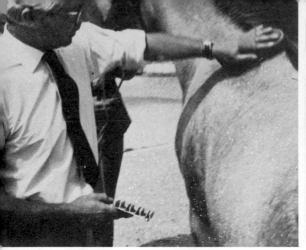

Grooming with the body brush

Cleaning the body brush on the curry comb

of it with the curry-comb, which is then tapped out on the floor. It is a common mistake among the uninformed that horses are groomed with the metal curry-comb, whereas its purpose is just to clean the brush. However, there are now rubber curry-combs, which can be used for brushing dried mud off the horse before grooming proper begins. Usually mud is brushed off with the dandy brush, which must always be used with care because it is made of hard, coarse bristle. Its main purpose is for brushing mud, dust and loose hairs from the winter coat of an unclipped horse.

Mane and Tail. These should be groomed with the water brush. It has long bristles, but is very much softer than the dandy brush, which is not suitable for the mane and tail, because it breaks the hairs. If you have no water brush, the body brush can be used instead. The well-groomed mane and tail of a stabled horse are easily kept smooth and free of tangles, and it may not be necessary to wet the brush. The full and long mane and tail natural to many ponies (and a valuable protection against flies and bad weather to any horse living out), or any neglected mane and tail need very patient brushing with a wet water brush, separating the tangles by hand. The tail can be dipped in a bucket of water (not the drinking bucket) and if very dirty washed in soapy water. The mane also can be washed occasionally if necessary,

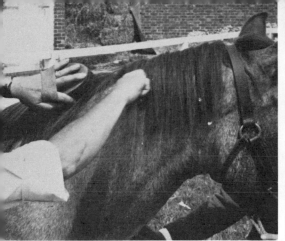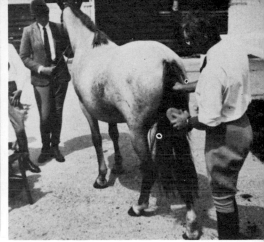

Grooming the mane and tail with the body brush

with soap or shampoo, not detergent. Never use a comb on mane or tail until all tangles have been brushed out.

For appearance only, and therefore quite unnecessary for ordinary purposes, the mane and tail can be trimmed by pulling, a skill best learned by watching an expert. The mane is thinned out, and reduced to an even length of 6 or 8 inches. You take a small bunch of hair in the fingers, back-comb to the length you want to keep, and pull out the longer hairs, very few at a time, with a sharp jerk. If there is much pulling to be done, or if your horse is at all unhappy about it, do the job gradually over a number of days, comforting him with some treat such as sugar. Never use scissors on the mane except, if it is to be plaited for a show, to remove the short mane hairs on the withers and at the poll under the head-piece of the bridle, in both cases to prevent any plaits pulling on those hairs.

Plaiting is purely for elegance, and it takes a long time and much practice to get a neat result. The well-brushed mane is divided into seven, or nine or more portions, each one is plaited evenly and secured $\frac{1}{2}$ inch ($1\frac{1}{2}$ cm.) from the end with strong thread of the same colour as the mane. Using a large darning-needle, double up the plait under itself and run a line of stitches through the plait, down it and up again, to make it flat and neat before fastening off at the top. Remember at the end of the day carefully to cut out the thread and undo the plaits: if left plaited for long the hair will be damaged.

49

Scissors are used to square the end of a tail, for appearance mainly and also to keep a long tail out of the mud. Since the tail is carried differently when the horse is moving from when he is standing still, you lift the top of the tail slightly upwards and away from the body, and then make a straight cut across the hairs not less than 6 inches (15 cm.) below the hocks. You may well need someone to help you.

Pulling the tail, for appearance only, is to achieve a slender tapered line. The natural line may be thought too bushy at the top, but a horse living out needs the full thickness of his tail for warmth. Hairs are pulled from the underside of the top 12 inches (30 cm.) of the tail, again using a comb and fingers, pulling a very few hairs at a time, choosing them to keep an even, smooth appearance. This is enhanced by brushing with a damp water brush, and further improved by the use of a tail bandage in the stable. The tail bandage must be dry. A wet bandage would shrink on drying and cause severe pain and damage to the tail, even the loss of it, and it is best not to leave the bandage on overnight. Starting at the top, wind the bandage firmly but not too tightly down the tail for about 12 inches (30 cm.), then wind it upwards again and tie the tapes at the top. It is much better that the bandage should fall off than that it should be too tight.

Feet. Shoeing will be dealt with in Chapter 7. Daily care of the feet consists in cleaning out each foot with the hoof-pick, working from heel to toe at least once a day, and preferably before and after exercise as well. It is most important in this way to prevent stable dirt and stones from outside remaining wedged in the crevices of the foot. Also by this daily inspection you watch for any injury to the foot or need for attention to the shoes. Unless daily care is made a regular habit it is easy for small troubles to become serious and even lead to permanent damage.

Clipping

In autumn horses and ponies shed the short smooth coat of summer and grow a winter coat, consisting of a short thick undercoat covered by long rain-shedding hair on the outside. Horses whose ancestors

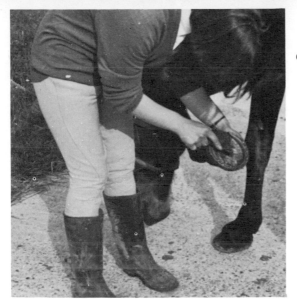

Cleaning out the fore foot

Full clip

Trace-high clip

came from warm climates, such as Arabs and their descendants the English Thoroughbreds, grow only light winter coats, compared with the wonderfully thick coats of some of the northern breeds, such as Siberian, Norwegian and Shetland ponies. Most horses are of mixed ancestry, with medium-thick winter coats.

A horse stabled in winter will benefit from the warmth of his natural coat if he is exercised only at slow paces so that he sweats hardly at all, but if hard or fast work is required of him he must be clipped. Otherwise he would first suffer from over-heating, and then from chill when his thick coat is soaked in cold sweat. A useful half-way measure is clipping trace-high, that is clipping only the lower part of the body. In any case the legs are always left unclipped, and the part of the back covered by the saddle. In Britain the first clipping is usually done about the end of October and then again about two months later. Sometimes a pony which has not been clipped in winter may be clipped in April if the weather is warm and the winter coat half-shed.

Clipping is not a job for the inexperienced, who in any case are not likely to own an electric clipping-machine or even an old one turned by hand. If not already nervous of the machine, a horse or pony may be made so by inexpert clipping, so it is best to have it done at a good riding establishment, where experienced people and the presence of other horses will prevent difficulties arising.

Rugs and Bandages

A clipped horse must be kept rugged in the stable, one rug for the day and another for the night, with one or more blankets under it according to the weather. A useful innovation is the sweat-rug made of wide-mesh nylon, worn underneath the woollen blanket and the horse-rug, which may be of wool-lined jute or of quilted nylon. When rugging up, that is putting on the blankets and rug, place them slightly forward, so that in pulling them back the hair is smoothed the right way. Do not let them drag on the withers, and secure them with a roller padded in the manner of saddle padding to avoid any pressure on the spine; fasten it much more loosely than a saddle girth.

For extra warmth in the stable, or for drying the legs after washing them if a horse comes in with legs soaked in mud, woollen bandages

Resting between events, showing (*left*) a fly sheet of netting and (*right*) exercise bandages for jumping

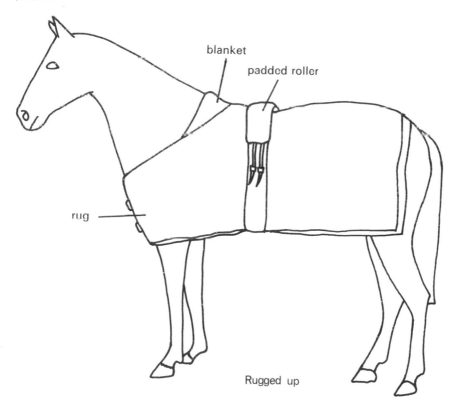

blanket

padded roller

rug

Rugged up

are wound round the legs from just below the knees and the hocks to cover the fetlocks. A thick padding of gamgee or cotton-wool protrudes above and below the bandages, which must not be wound tightly. If the legs are wet, the padding must be changed after an hour or so. Exercise bandages are similar, except that they must not cover the fetlocks, and often they are applied to the front legs only. Their purpose is to protect the tendons from jarring, particularly when jumping or at exercise on hard ground.

A horse kept stabled in summer may be glad of a fly-sheet, a very light cotton rug to protect him from flies: also it keeps his coat smooth and clean if he has been prepared for a show.

Exercise and Rest

It is important to allow an hour for digestion before exercise. You should always walk your horse for the first ten minutes to warm up his muscles and so avoid strains; never canter on hard roads, only on soft going such as grass or sand. Gallop only occasionally, when well warmed up and on soft ground. If at all hot, you should walk as long as is necessary to bring your horse in cool, whether this takes ten minutes or half an hour. If you cannot avoid bringing him in hot, then either you must lead him about until he cools, or, for instance if it is raining, put him in the stable after covering his back first with a bundle of hay and then a rug over that. When he is cool, brush off the hay and rug him up if it is winter. If he has had a long hard ride, you should go back to him an hour or two later in case he has broken out in a sweat again, as can happen and lead to serious chilling.

Long walks do more to improve a horse's condition than shorter rides trotting or cantering. When a horse is brought in from summer grazing to be stabled for the winter, he should be walked daily for several weeks before being allowed first to trot and then to canter.

If snow and frost make riding impossible, you should either lead your horse about for at least half an hour twice a day, or lunge him in a circle after putting down peat or straw. Lungeing is described in Chapter 6. But much the best way, if you are lucky enough to have one near by, is to borrow or hire the use of an indoor school. In countries where snow is usual, horses are shod with special shoes to prevent them slipping on packed snow, whether being ridden or pulling sleighs.

The amount of work a horse can do depends on his condition, which is described in Chapter 7, but whatever his condition may be it is important for him to have sufficient rest. It is natural for a horse to sleep standing up for short rests several times a day, and he should have breaks in his work for this. For a good night's rest he should lie down comfortably, in a stable if it is winter or the weather is bad. He should have time to feed during the day, for it is not fair to work a horse all day and then expect him to seek his food by grazing all night instead of sleeping.

A horse in soft condition should do only light work. Under-nourished horses and ponies and those being worked when too young or too old tire very quickly, especially in hot climates.

Children sharing a pony, whether their own or hired, must be careful not to overwork him, particularly when competing in gymkhanas. It is not fair on the pony to enter him in every class, and he should be given time during the day to rest in the shade, with a hay-net and after a drink of water. The girths should be loosened (remember to tighten them again) or the saddle removed if the weather is warm enough to be sure his back will not be chilled if it is sweaty. If he travelled in a horse-box, it may be best to rest him in that, away from the flies. Except for warming him up, and going over a few low practice jumps if he is to jump, you should keep off his back between events, to save his strength. If you ride to and from the show-ground, allow plenty of time, to average not more than 6 miles an hour, and if you have a long way to go, get off and walk occasionally. Besides getting up early in the morning to allow for the hour's digestion after feeding, you may have to leave before the end of the show to get home before dark. Horses are in great danger on dark roads, and red stirrup lamps should be carried in case you are late. On a long day's trek, keep to slow paces, and give your horse a long midday rest with water and some light food, either grazing, hay, or horse-nuts.

Tack

This word describes the leather and metal equipment you need for a riding horse, the saddle and bridle and headcollar. The advantage of a headcollar rather than a halter is that the headcollar can be left on a horse out at grass if he is one that is difficult to catch, whereas a halter must never be left on because the webbing shrinks when wet.

Tack need not be bought new; well-kept second-hand saddles and bridles may even be better than new ones since they are more supple. Uncared for, cracked leather is worse than useless, even if not very old. New leather needs much care in making it supple.

New or second-hand, you have to decide what type of saddle and bridle you need, and then to see that they fit your horse or pony perfectly.

Bridles. These, and headcollars too, come in three main sizes, pony, cob (large pony) and full size. The bridle is adjustable as to the cheek-piece and throat-lash, and the important thing is to see that the brow-band is not too tight. The nose-band is separate from the rest of the bridle, and is sometimes dispensed with, but it is necessary for attaching a standing martingale if one is used, and also for attaching a lead-ing-rein for a child learning to ride or competing in a leading-rein show class.

The choice of a bit has been made a complicated subject, but there are only three main types to consider, the snaffle, pelham and double bridle (of bit and bridoon).

The Snaffle. As a beginner you should never use anything but a snaffle, and if you are not able to control your pony with this bit, ignore any old-fashioned advice that you need a stronger bit, as that would only make matters worse. What you need is more practice in an enclosed space, or on a leading-rein, or with an easier pony.

Since a horse can attempt to resist a snaffle by opening his mouth, a drop nose-band is often used, which by passing round the nose and under the rings of the bit holds the mouth shut, and it can be useful when extra control is needed for a short time, such as during a round of show-jumping. To prevent its use from being abused, great care is needed to be sure that it is not too tight, and that the cheek-strap of the nose-band is adjusted to a length which keeps the front of the drop nose-band above the soft lower part of the muzzle under which there is no bone, where any pressure would be painful and likely to restrict breathing. Obviously it is preferable to be able to control your horse without this device.

The Pelham. Whereas the snaffle bit is usually jointed in the middle, giving it a slightly pincer action in the mouth, the pelham has a single bar, straight or slightly curved (called half-moon) made of steel or vulcanite, and with cheek-pieces to take a second pair of reins, and hooks for a curb-chain. Like the drop nose-band, it is often used to give increased control, and sometimes for young children or for show-jumping a single pair of reins is used (to avoid having two pairs to handle), attached to short loops of strap joining the bit ring and the cheek-piece ring. It is most important to learn the correct fitting of the curb-chain, as described in Chapter 1. If it is too loose it has no effect, and if it is too tight it causes great pain. The pelham has been largely replaced by the snaffle with drop nose-band, since it is not a bit for beginners who may accidentally jerk the reins. An experienced rider would prefer a double bridle, which gives accurate control in advanced equitation.

Snaffle bridle with ordinary nose-band and a lead rein attached to a loop joining the snaffle rings

Snaffle bridle with drop nose-band and running martingale

The Double Bridle. This is made up of two separate bits, the bridoon which is a snaffle, and a curb bit, of which there are several varieties. This is the bit for advanced riders, and it is seen in the show ring and in *haute ecole* (advanced dressage), where it is the means of giving very delicate control of precise movements. You should not use it until you have a really independent seat, which means that your body position is so well controlled as not to affect the position of your hands.

Martingales. These are for the purpose of giving extra control of a horse's head.

The standing martingale is for a horse which is inclined to throw his head up, which could make him difficult to control, or knock the rider on the head. It consists of a strap running from the underside of the nose-band through a slot in a neck-strap to the girth. The strap must be long enough to give the horse sufficient freedom of head movement, particularly for jumping, when he needs to stretch his neck. The standing martingale must be attached to an ordinary nose-band, not to a drop nose-band.

The running martingale is attached to the reins, not the nose-band. It has two straps, with rings through which the snaffle reins pass (never the curb reins), and therefore its action is controlled through

Pelham bridle with ordinary nose-band and standing martingale

Pelham bridle with single rein

the rider's hands. Its length must be such that with normal head carriage the reins run in a straight line from the bit to the rider's hand.

The Irish martingale, often seen on racehorses, is a short strap with rings at either end through which the snaffle reins pass, and it has the effect of keeping the reins in place if a horse throws his head about.

A beginner should not be riding a pony which needs a martingale at all.

Saddles. These come in different shapes, sizes and qualities, and they must fit the horse or pony and be comfortable for the rider.

Numnah Saddles. A small broad-backed pony, although really unsuitable, is often a child's first mount, and sometimes the only saddle likely to fit him is a felt saddle or numnah. It is entirely flexible, and so brings the same disadvantages as bareback riding that the rider's weight rests on the pony's spine. Also, to prevent the numnah slipping forward, which it is likely to do on a fat pony, it is often fitted with a crupper, which may be helpful with a slow pony. But when an active pony slows down or stops suddenly, the pull or jerk under his tail makes him buck, a natural reaction for which he cannot be blamed. Felt saddles are too flexible for it to be practicable to fit safety bars for suspending the stirrups, and so it is necessary to use safety stirrup irons, as described in Chapter 1, to be sure that a foot cannot be caught in the stirrup when the child falls off.

Leather Saddles. These are made in a number of sizes as to both width and length or can be made to measure. In the larger sizes there is also a choice of shape, from the show type, the flaps cut very straight in front to show off the forehand to advantage, through the general purpose type, to show-jumping saddles with the flaps curved forwards and a roll of padding to keep the rider's knees in position. The importance of fitting the saddle to the horse has been described in Chapter 1. From the rider's point of view the saddle needs to be large enough for his length of thigh, and its balance must be right, the lowest point in the middle, not towards the back, which would tip him on to the cantle. Ask for a Pony Club approved saddle, designed for the correct balance.

Saddles may be lined with cloth, which wears out, or leather, which does not. The saddle tree, on to which the leather and padding are built, used to be of wood, which is easily broken, but now is usually of metal and can be designed to be springy, for the rider's comfort. For the horse's comfort a sheepskin numnah can be worn under the saddle. The use of a saddle cloth is either for appearance or to keep the saddle lining clean and, as mentioned in Chapter 1, it is no substitute for proper saddle padding. The saddle cloth should be pulled well up above the withers, to make sure it cannot press down on them.

Western Saddle. The Western style of riding was adopted by cowboys who have to endure long hours in the saddle and to perform exacting work, such as steer-roping. They also have to carry equipment. The large saddle with high pommel and cantle gives stability to the rider, and the bridle with curb-bit and single pair of reins held in one hand allows control of the horse with one hand free for action. The horse must be trained to respond to neck-reining, that is turning to left or right according to light pressure on the neck as the rider swings his hand across the withers. The rider must have a perfectly independent seat, and ride on a loose rein except when he makes contact with the bit to slow or stop. The horse must be trained to stand perfectly still when the rider dismounts, because with the high cantle he leaves his left foot in the stirrup while swinging his right leg to the ground.

Western riding is often popular for pleasure riding, since the rider appreciates the feeling of security in the saddle. But there is risk of hurting the horse's mouth by an accidental jerk on the strong bit, which is suitable only for experienced riders. Also the large rigid saddle, necessarily cushioned for the horse by a thick saddle blanket, prevents communication from the rider's seat, which is an important aid in equitation. For these reasons Western riding, apart from professional cowboys, is suitable for trail-riding, but less suitable for ordinary pleasure riding or for learning to ride.

Care of Tack. All tack must be cleaned every time you use it. Apart from appearance, unless leather straps are first made supple and then kept so, they become dry, cracked and liable to snap. A broken bridle,

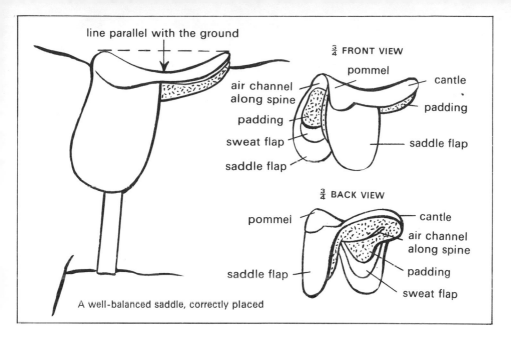

line parallel with the ground

¾ FRONT VIEW

pommel

cantle

air channel along spine

padding

padding

sweat flap

saddle flap

saddle flap

¾ BACK VIEW

pommel

cantle

air channel along spine

saddle flap

padding

sweat flap

A well-balanced saddle, correctly placed

rein or stirrup leather can be disastrous to the rider, and a dirty saddle lining or girth can cause sores to the horse.

The routine after unsaddling is first to see to your horse. Rub the saddle mark on his back with straw, or let him out in the field to roll. Then with clean water rinse the bit and sponge off any mud from bridle, saddle and stirrups. Use warm water and saddle soap to remove grease from any straps such as stirrup leathers and leather saddle lining: a cloth saddle lining is cleaned by brushing. Now with a sponge or cloth only slightly damp, apply saddle soap to all the leather, and as it dries polish it off with a dry cloth. At least once a week all buckles must be undone, to soap thoroughly every leather part of the bridle, stirrups, reins and the flaps and girth straps of the saddle. Leather girths are kept soft with neat's foot oil, and the cloth which is folded into them should be kept soaked in oil. Oil is also helpful in softening any stiff new leather, though it darkens the colour.

Spurs. The only proper use for spurs is as a precision aid in advanced equitation. Used delicately in this way they should not cause pain, and they give a signal more accurately timed than from leg pressure alone. Obviously the use of spurs can be and often is an abuse, and children should never be allowed to wear them. You may hear it argued that blunt spurs (without rowels) are harmless, and when gently used by riders perfectly in control of their leg movements this can be true, but blunt spurs can and do cause severe bruising. They should not be used to coerce an inadequately trained horse, or as a substitute for learning how to achieve impulsion from the rider's legs and back.

Whips.   If you want to carry a whip, it should be a short light one, such as a leather-covered cane. The whip used to be necessary for side-saddle riders as an aid instead of the leg and heel on the off-side. It should never be used in gymkhana events, nor for urging a tired horse and least of all for punishment. If his horse has made some mistake, a good horseman blames himself and tries to discover what he did wrong.

Western tack

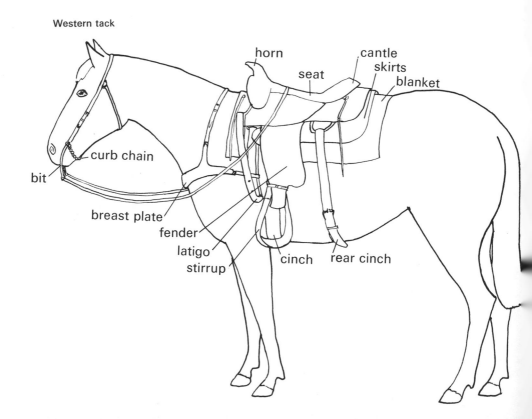

5 Living Out

IN BRITAIN MOST CHILDREN's ponies and many horses live out of doors, living on grass in summer, supplemented with hay for the winter half of the year, and with the addition of concentrates, mainly grain and horse-nuts, in quantities according to the amount of work to be done. The British Isles, and particularly Ireland, are fortunate in having a mild and moist climate which keeps the grass growing for many months in the year, whereas in many parts of the world the grass fails in summer from heat and drought as well as from cold in winter. In the dry grassland regions of the world horses such as the famous Arabians of the Middle East, the wild horses of Central Asia and the horses of the North and South American plains and of Australia all thrive in a wild state so long as they can roam over vast areas to find what food and water there is.

Hot wet equatorial regions are not suitable for horses living out. The rain washes the goodness out of the soil, so that the natural grass is coarse and lacking in nourishment and when finer grasses are sown they do not flourish. It is sad to see the suffering in the heat of debilitated horses originally introduced by Europeans to equatorial countries.

The Field

To keep a horse or pony out at grass you need a field of at least two acres per animal. If you have a farm or estate, choose a field of good pasture on well-drained land, and see that it is suitably fenced and provided with water. Good pasture has grass and other edible plants such as clover growing so thickly that no bare earth can be seen, and it should be regularly grazed (or mown) so that fresh young shoots grow all the time in spring and summer. Thin pasture on poor soils and coarse pasture on swamp-land are unsuitable for horses although they may be adequate for moorland pony breeds. On neglected pasture the coarse grasses and broad-leaved plants destroy the finer grasses by overshadowing them so that they die out, leaving bare, patches to be colonised by more weeds. A field which has been cut for hay is likely to need time for young shoots to grow again before it is fit for grazing, and a field to which fertiliser has been applied is unfit for horses, and more especially for ponies, for at least three weeks, which must include a period of rain. If you have no good pasture of your own, there may be a suitable field near to your home which the owner will rent to you by the year, or which he will allow your pony to share with other animals, horses or cows, for a weekly sum.

It is no use trying to keep a horse or pony out at grass all the time in a small paddock, because although you will expect to buy hay for winter, and for summer too in times of drought, the turf will be so much cut up by trampling hooves, impoverished by over-grazing (not letting the grass have a chance to grow) and fouled by excreta that it will soon be ruined. The best use for a small paddock is for part-time grazing and natural exercise for a mainly stable-kept animal, or as a home paddock for one living mainly on hired grazing.

In any field or paddock of only about two acres per animal, the droppings should as far as possible be removed. Horses normally avoid fouling their pasture and leave their droppings at the edge of the field or on a patch which has already been fouled; unless regularly cleared of droppings, the fouled patches and edges will spread. They may be obviously useless and covered in coarse weeds and nettles, or they may appear as lush dark green grass, which the horses know to be bad for them, and so will starve rather than graze it. This is because all horses carry the eggs of parasitic worms, most of them invisible to the naked eye, and these worms are spread by horse droppings in long grass. Where the grass is short, the worm eggs may be killed by strong sunshine, so by removing droppings regularly, and repeatedly cutting any rank patches or edges, they may in time be restored to good grazing. But where a whole paddock or field through over-stocking with horses has become horse-sick, as this fouled pasture is called, or if the grass has become sparse and weedy through over-grazing, the best course is to re-seed with quality pasture grasses. This can be done in winter and spring by the usual ploughing and cultivating, or in summer by applying paraquat which kills the grass and weeds quickly, leaving the ground ready for sowing after cultivating only.

However large or small your field may be, you can prevent it becoming horse-sick by regularly resting it from horses. This can be achieved by means of a dividing fence, the resting half being cleared of dung and the grass left to grow strong again, though the pony may have to be hay-fed meanwhile. In a large field the droppings should be spread by chain-harrowing, and if there is more grass than your horse needs the pasture will benefit by taking a hay crop from it. Or you may keep cattle on it for a while, since they keep the grass evenly short, and cow dung fertilises the ground without souring it. Horses graze happily in a field with cattle.

Fencing

A much higher standard of fencing is needed for horses than for cattle. For one thing, they can jump, some of them 5 feet (1½ metres) or more, and also they gallop about and chase each other, and these are two reasons for avoiding the use of barbed-wire. Apalling injuries are caused by accidental entanglement and terrified struggling in barbed-wire. Posts and plain wire can be used if the posts are very secure, and at least four strands of wire fixed taut by means of a strainer. Horses and especially ponies are inclined to find a way through ordinary wire fencing, and once they have found a weak place

Post and rails fencing

Water trough with piped supply

they will work at it to loosen it however often it is repaired. So it is well worth your while to start with well made secure fencing, high enough and strong enough for all circumstances, even such difficult ones as a mare in season, one pony left behind while its companion is taken out riding, or hay-fed animals in bare pasture longing for the young corn in the next field.

The best fencing is wooden post and rails, the posts planted by a mechanical pile-driver. Instead of the three or four wooden rails, or under one top-rail, you can use thick square-mesh pig- or sheep-wire. For ponies a height 4 foot 6 inches ($1\frac{1}{2}$ metres) is necessary and for horses at least 5 feet ($1\frac{1}{2}$ metres). A thick hedge of thorn can make a good fence, especially if it is a laid hedge; if not laid, a single strand of thick wire may be needed in case a gap should appear.

Gates should be wide for convenience in leading horses through, and as strong as the fencing, preferably with two sets of fastenings of a type which clever ponies cannot undo with their mouths. If trespassers may leave a gate unfastened a chain and padlock are necessary and if there is a right of way there should be a style beside the gate.

Water

A reliable supply of water is essential, and a shallow clear natural stream with no risk of chemical pollution is ideal. Where a stream or river is too deep or the bank too steep for safety, it is often possible to dig out a shallow creek or bay, back from the river into the field, with gentle slopes where ponies may drink safely. A stagnant pond or ditch, without a stream flowing through, is not good drinking-water for horses and should be fenced off. Then piped water must be used, the most convenient way being permanent pipes leading to a trough, which must be cleaned out once a week; if not supplied automatically it must be filled up daily. If there are no fixed pipes, you may be able to run a length of hose from a tap or standpipe to the field. For one or two ponies only, water can be carried in buckets, but remember that a pony sometimes needs several three gallon buckets of water in a day, and must never be short of water. They are thirsty not only in hot weather, but also in winter when living on dry food, and then also it is important to remember to break the ice as often as necessary.

Shelter

Horses and ponies in the wild know where to find shelter from wind or driving rain from any direction. They make use of woodland, copses, hills and valleys, rocks and gullies, standing close together, heads low and tails to the wind. Those with thick winter coats can withstand both snow and dry cold, and they move about to restore warmth. Heavy rain on their thin summer coats distresses them and they will gallop for the shelter of a tree. Their worst trouble is flies, biting, stinging and clustering on the eyelids until they become sore and infected. Horses seem to know instinctively that the bot and warble flies (which lay eggs which hatch into parasitic maggots) must not be allowed to settle, and so there is not a moment's peace when one is about: they look rather like a honey-bee. By standing head to tail, even in sunlight the flies can be kept moving, or the horses may seek shelter in shady places largely free of flies.

A field may have reasonable shelter if it is surrounded by thick, high hedges, giving a choice of shelter from any direction. Banks and walls are less useful, as they tend to produce draughts and eddies. Low-trimmed hedges, rails or wire give no protection at all, whether from winter winds, autumn rains or summer flies, and a shelter must be provided. It may be a simple wooden shed of a size suitable for the number of animals using it, with one long side largely open for easy access and to avoid kicking. For one horse it should measure not less than 12 × 10 feet (3½ by 3 metres) with a roof 10 feet (3 metres) high, sloping from front to back. The open side should face the least bad weather, according to the local climate, and if the shelter stands away from the field fence, the horses can stand behind it when shelter is needed from the opposite direction. The field shelter can be built of wooden posts and weather boarding, and roofed with felt over boards; corrugated iron is not so good because it gives no insulation against heat and cold, and is noisy in rain. Prefabricated shelters can be bought in several sizes.

Better than a field shelter is to have a fenced way running between field and stable to give access at any time, or if you have no stable, to build one in the field. As mentioned in Chapter 4, at times of illness, injury or too much grass it is essential for horses to be stabled; prefabricated stables which you can buy are also mentioned. For economy

A field shelter

Mid-day in summer: ponies
protecting one another from flies

you may prefer to build one yourself, but do get an experienced
builder to help you or it may not be strong enough; serious accidents
to horses have resulted from the collapse of home-made stables. The
builder will know how to lay the concrete and plant the uprights
securely, giving a height of at least 10 feet (3 metres) at the front end
and a bit less at the back; he will know how to fix the rafters and the
felt roofing, how to fill in the sides with boards, with a divided door to
each loose-box and louvred ventilation high up in the back or side
wall. Choose a site as well-drained, sheltered and level as possible, and
measure out the ground plan according to the number of loose-boxes
you want, about 12 by 10 feet ($3\frac{1}{2}$ by 3 metres) for horses, or 10 × 8
feet (3 by $2\frac{1}{2}$ metres) for ponies. The concrete should extend a yard
(metre) or so in front of the stable and can be scored with criss-cross
lines to prevent slipping. If drainage channels are made in the concrete,
the drains should lead to a sump behind the stable. Guttering fixed
to collect the rain-water can provide a useful supply to a trough or

A horse or pony out at grass needs a companion   . . . if only a donkey

tub. It is usually convenient to include a tack-room and forage store, which also helps to insulate the stable.

Whether home-made or prefabricated, a stable in the field saves the owner a great deal of time, since by leaving the stable doors open, your horse or pony can take shelter at will. Where there are several ponies, each will know his own loose-box, and if one has to be shut in for any reason he will have the company of the others grazing near by.

If they are fed out in the field instead of bringing them into the stable for feeding, it is important to put their hay-nets or piles of hay and their buckets of horse-nuts well apart, or there is likely to be kicking and bullying.

Company

Horses and ponies have an instinctive need of company, just as we have, being like us social animals. If you can only keep one horse or pony you may be able to share grazing with friends, keeping both animals alternately in their field and yours. Or you may be able to keep a donkey or goat for company, though fencing to hold a goat can be a problem; cows are better than nothing. But what your horse or pony really needs is another of his own kind for companionship, and stimulus to take exercise running and playing together, as well as for mutual protection from flies.

69

Supervision

Horses and ponies out at grass do not need the time-consuming attention essential when they are stable-kept, but it is a mistake to suppose that you can just turn them into a field and leave them. Most of the time all will be well, but a proper daily inspection is needed at all times, every day of the year. You must check on food, water, hoof condition and fencing, and watch for any injury from kicks or thorns or stones in the feet, and for any illness, minor or serious, as described in Chapter 7. In checking the food supply you need to watch the condition of your horse or pony as well as of the grass. In spring even grass that is fairly short may be too nourishing for a pony, not only making him too fat, but risking damage to his feet through laminitis (described in Chapter 7). To prevent this it may be essential to shut him in the stable for several hours every day. In Britain from October to April it is the opposite: there may seem to be plenty of grass, but as it is lacking in nourishment at this season additional hay or concentrates are necessary for good health.

For this daily inspection obviously it is easier for you if the field is close to your home, and a horse or pony living alone needs your company close at hand. Also if the field is out of sight there is the danger that he may be stolen, or hurt by hooligans throwing stones.

Grooming

To prevent sores it is essential to brush the saddle and girth areas before riding, and for appearance you will want to brush away loose hairs and mud and to keep the mane and tail free of tangles. If your pony does a lot of work he may need more grooming than this, with body brush in summer and dandy brush in winter. This is to keep the skin healthy by removing the excess grease caused by sweating, but when living out enough grease must be left in the coat for protection against rain and cold, particularly in winter. He will, of course, have his natural thick coat in winter, and in spring, when this is being shed, it is important to brush him every day. Otherwise the irritation may distress him and he may even rub sores trying to scratch himself on trees and fencing. If he is muddy do not wash him, but brush off the mud after it has dried, and be sure to dry a wet back before riding.

70

As with the stabled horse, you should clean out his feet before and after riding, and inspect them regularly even when he is not being ridden at all, to be sure they are healthy; for instance a feeling of heat in the hoof is a warning either of an infected injury or of laminitis, described in Chapter 7, and you need the vet. When turned out to grass for any length of time without work it is good for the feet to remove the shoes. The importance of regular care of the feet, whether shod or unshod, is also described in Chapter 7.

Management: In or Out

This and the previous chapter describing the care of horses and ponies in the stable and living out at grass show what is necessary in each case in terms of accommodation, feeding and time spent in daily care. Where grass is available and the climate suitable it is much easier and cheaper to have your horse living out, but where little or no grazing is available he may have to be stabled, in your own stable, one rented near by, or at livery. Apart from this, there are other points to consider. He will have to be stabled if he needs to be grain-fed for high performance, for instance in show-jumping. In winter a horse doing hard work of any kind must live in, because his coat must be clipped for work and then he needs to be kept warm with rugs in the stable. Even unclipped horses if thoroughbred, Arabian or three-quarter bred are likely to have coats much too thin to live out in winter in Britain, which has milder winters than many other countries. The New Zealand rug is waterproof and has straps to go round the hind-legs to keep it in place, and it is useful for allowing a stabled horse to take walking exercise in a paddock by day. It is not advisable to keep a horse out day and night in a New Zealand rug because it becomes heavy and sodden if there is much rain and may become displaced, for instance by rolling, and cause sores, and even with the necessary daily change of rug and grooming the coat is likely to suffer. Horses and ponies which thrive outside during the summer will benefit from being kept in at night in winter, and there is also the advantage that the grazing will not be so much damaged by trampling.

If for convenience and cheapness you decide that your horse or pony must live out all the year, it can be the happiest way for both of you. But you must remember the limitations on what you ask of him in work and performance, on the type of animal you choose, the need for shelter and the importance of daily attention to all his needs. For all horses and ponies it is best to have both stables and grazing, if only a small paddock for the stabled horse or a home-made stable for the grass-kept pony.

(*Above and below*) Ponies in winter coats

Living out in winter coat with shoes removed

6 Training

Mind and Body

You may wonder why a chapter on training comes in a handbook for the inexperienced, since the training of a horse is a matter for experts, and much harm can be done to a young horse if his initial training is attempted by anyone lacking the necessary skill and patience. The old expression was "breaking and making"; breaking means accustoming a horse to be handled and controlled and making means training him to understand and respond to the aids. The word training includes the two aspects of conditioning the horse's mind and also the conditioning of his body so that he is able as well as willing to do what is asked of him.

A horse's mental powers of acute observation and accurate memory make it possible to train him to remember and to react to a system of signals called the aids, and, as has already been mentioned in Chapter 1 on handling, these mental powers also mean that everything you do with your horse, whether mounted or on foot, is noticed by him and remembered. If what you do corresponds with what he learned from his trainer in the first place, you reinforce his tendency to right behaviour. But if you do not trouble to ride him in the right way, he is likely to find ways of following his own inclinations instead of yours. A well-mannered horse or pony, one which behaves in a controlled way and responds quickly to your aids, can soon be made nappy by weak or careless riding. Nappy means the opposite of well-mannered, refusing to do as you ask. Perhaps worst of all, by carelessness you may let him discover that he is so much stronger than you that he can get his own way by force. Then if you try to correct these difficulties with roughness or anger instead of with tact and patient skill, you may spoil his temper as well. All this explains why every rider and horse-owner should have some knowledge of the right way to train a horse, and it brings us again to the point made in Chapter 3 that a beginner should buy a horse or pony of placid temperament and old enough to be well set in ways of good behaviour. It is true that some animals put up with outrageous mishandling by children and others, but also it is not surprising that many have learned bad ways, either through weak, incompetent riding, or through trying to protect themselves from such abuses as rough handling and over-riding. The earlier chapters in this book have shown you how to handle your pony in the quiet way which suits his nature best, how to learn and practice good riding with expert tuition and how to develop and maintain your pony's physical fitness by good feeding and exercise.

Following on from this, as an owner responsible for your horse in every way, you will want to improve his capabilities as well as your own. For this you need to understand the sequence of his training, and to repeat parts of it throughout his life.

Lungeing

Obedience to control by rein and voice is first taught by lungeing, sending the young horse or pony round on a long rein in a circle. If he has always had plenty of good food and opportunities to play and gallop he will have good muscles, whereas one whose inadequate feeding, confinement in a small space or loneliness has discouraged his taking much spontaneous exercise must be restored to good condition before any training begins. Apart from good or bad condition, a young horse is always to some extent unbalanced in that he puts more than half his weight on the fore-hand, the part of his body in front of the withers, and he lacks the muscular tone for quick changes in direction, speed or pace. These physical qualities are improved gradually by lungeing, preparing him to be able to adjust his balance while carrying a rider, and it is very wrong to attempt to ride a youngster which has not been conditioned in this way, and lungeing should not begin until the horse or pony is three years old.

A long rein, about 20 feet (6 metres), of webbing or cord is attached to the headcollar, or more correctly to a cavesson, which is a head-collar with a ring to take the rein on the front of the nose-band, and you take your pony to a flat piece of ground, not less than about half a tennis court in size. If it is fenced in, if only on one or two sides, so much the better. To lunge on the left rein, you lead him forward on a left-handed circle, gradually letting out the rein through your left hand as you drop back beside his quarters and away from him. With a whip, or a long flexible willow stick will do, pointing to his quarters and saying "Walk on" encourage him to keep moving forwards on the circle, till he learns to keep at the distance you choose, anything from 10 to 20 feet (3 to 6 metres), while you stand still in the middle. You teach him to stop by saying "Whoa", at first holding the whip in front of him, until he understands. Change from one circle to the other every few minutes, and give praise and an occasional reward. When he is reliable at the walk, get him to trot, by word and signal with the whip—there should be no need to touch him with it—and encourage him to settle into a rhythmical stride. Again change the circle frequently, and practice starting, walking, trotting, walking and stopping again. Do not attempt the canter until the trot is reliable, and never let him go faster than a moderate canter.

Being on a circle, he is likely to strike off with the correct foot, the inner fore-foot, but if he does not, check him and start him again. Most horses prefer the left circle, being slightly stiff on the right side, so you should notice on which circle he goes the more easily and practice more on the other. In this way the young animal learns to start, stop and change pace by word of command only, and all the time improves his strength, suppleness and balance. He learns to walk actively with long strides, then to trot with spring and rhythm, and finally to canter smoothly, leading with the correct foot, well balanced by bringing his hind-legs forward under his body as he moves. If he was thoroughly and skilfully lunged as a three year old, you will find no difficulty in lungeing him again; he will understand at once. Remember to change circle frequently, to alternate faster paces with walking, and not to bore him with long sessions; twenty minutes to half an hour is enough at a time.

It is useful for any owner to know how to lunge for several reasons. A horse may need exercise in freezing slippery weather, when you can lunge him on a circular track covered in straw or sand; or when, regrettably, a saddle sore, girth gall or sore mouth prevents you riding him. He may need gradual re-conditioning after recovery from illness or accident, or just after a long spell out at grass. Or you may yourself be unable to ride for some reason. Another use for lungeing is that parents can exercise small ponies, which often need the edge taken off their exuberance before being ridden by young children. Again, parents who do not ride can by lungeing exercise a school child's pony during the week to have it fit for a long ride or a gymkhana at the week-end, and towards the end of term to prepare it for active riding in the school holidays.

Long-reining

The next stage in training is to teach your horse to move forwards responding to signals from a long pair of reins attached to a bit in the horse's mouth, and reaching the trainer's hands through rings on a roller or surcingle. Only an expert should attempt to do this, even with a horse already trained, so it will not now be described in detail.

Backing

This means mounting a horse for the first time, and he needs first to get used to the feel of a saddle on his back. To begin with it should just be placed on his back, then girthed loosely, later very carefully girthed up properly, and it is helpful, too, to lean on his back and to put a little weight in the stirrup several times before actually mounting. Then, when he is used to the saddle, with someone else holding his bridle, the trainer mounts quietly and sits still for a while before letting the horse move forward. A young horse should be backed only by an experienced rider, who gives confidence by moving smoothly and by being able to stay in the saddle if the horse reacts by bucking; falling off would frighten him. He should not be backed until he is at least three years old, and then should be ridden gently until he is four. He does not reach his full strength till he is five or six years old, and overworking young horses leads to lameness and back trouble at the time and in later life.

Schooling

The horse's training now continues from the saddle, with daily lungeing as well. The trainer uses the words of command which the horse now knows, while simultaneously applying the aids for starting, stopping and change of pace till the words are no longer needed. At the same time the horse is learning to respond to the pressures of the trainer's hands and legs by which he is kept in a straight line or turned. At first walking, then trotting and cantering, his obedience, understanding, strength and suppleness are developed by riding in circles, in straight lines with sharp turns at the corners of the ground, serpentines and figures of eight, stopping, backing (this time meaning walking backwards in a straight line) and moving forward again, with changes of speed and of pace. The skilled trainer with gentle hands and firm legs will teach him to flex at the poll, that is bend his neck just behind his head, and relax his jaw, so that he responds to the lightest touch on the reins. Only the best riding schools have ponies trained to go light in hand like this, and you need expert advice in training yourself and your pony to this standard. It is very well worth while achieving this flexion and lightness, because it is this which gives easy control and the joy of riding as one with your horse.

Daily practice at these schooling exercises is excellent for your riding progress as well as for your horse, so long as you try to perform each movement as near to perfection as you can. Ride up and down slopes as well as on the flat, even up and down steep banks so long as you keep your horse at right angles to the slope, so that any slipping will not cause a fall. As you progress, your horse will become increasingly handy, which means able and willing to move exactly as you ask of him, for instance starting into a canter from a halt and "turning on a sixpence", and you will be refining your aids until they are almost imperceptible to an onlooker. In emergency, such as another pony at a gymkhana running back at him to kick him, you can move him quickly out of danger, and his confidence in you will enable you to soothe him in case of accident or illness. This schooling practice is also the basis for success in every kind of competitive riding.

Gymkhanas

Besides general schooling, you and your pony will need practice in the particular events you want to enter, and it helps if you can practise with friends. For bending races, set up wooden poles, not metal or bamboo which are dangerous when you knock into them, placing them in rows with regular spacing and weave in and out of them. Begin slowly, ride correctly, and work up to speed with practice. Other skills you may want to practise are bareback riding, leaping into the saddle—or bareback without using a stirrup, starting, turning and stopping quickly, control of speed between slow and fast, and trotting fast without breaking into a canter.

77

Jumping

Horses and ponies in the wild seldom jump, preferring to go through water and round obstacles, but when galloping from danger, or in play, they will jump natural obstacles. So all horses can be trained to jump small fences (the word for any artificial obstacle for jumping), many can develop considerable jumping ability and just a few reach the top in show-jumping or steeplechasing. Success depends not only on natural ability and good physical condition but also very much on the skill of the rider. The wise trainer avoids tiring or boring his horse with too much practice, and above all he avoids over-facing him, that is asking him to jump a fence which at the moment is beyond his powers. While practising keep the fences lower than those you hope to jump in the show-ring, even though he is able to jump bigger ones. He will become confident that he is able to clear any fence you ask him to. He will not be likely to refuse to jump or to run out sideways for fear of bruising his legs by hitting a pole, or of jarring them as he lands from a height. Jarring of the fore-legs is another reason for not practising too much; on landing one of his fore-feet always momentarily takes all his weight and yours. So long as he enjoys jumping he will continue to improve, and if he becomes unwilling, possibly through an unlucky accident while jumping, you will need great patience in restoring his confidence, starting again from the beginning with very small fences.

The initial training for jumping consist of first walking, then trotting and finally cantering over poles laid on the ground. The next stage is jumping small solid obstacles scarcely 18 inches ($\frac{1}{2}$ metre) high, as you did when learning at your riding school. With your own horse or pony you should begin in the same way, spacing a series of low fences at a distance convenient to his stride. You ride calmly and rhythmically, holding him straight at the fence and urging him over them. He will be practising the placing of his feet and his timing, gaining confidence that you will not jab him in the mouth, bump down on his back or fall over his head on landing. Gradually you increase the size of the practice fences, but never beyond a size both of you can manage easily, and making them always at least as wide from front to back as they are high. This is so that he will jump in the way natural to a horse, in a wide arc, arching his back and lifting his hind-feet. If he jumps with a flat or hollow back his hind-legs are likely to catch the fence, and trying to jump at a steep angle puts a great strain on the hocks. The landing side of each fence must be soft ground, which in dry weather means spreading a thick wide layer of peat or sand. It is not necessary to buy expensive fences, and you can improvise by supporting poles on old oil drums, boxes or other home made supports, so long as you make sure that the pole can be easily knocked down, and if it can fall in one direction only, be sure not to jump it from the wrong side. Some of the poles can be painted white, or in black-and-white stripes. Since the horse's sight is different from ours, it is believed that he cannot recognise the bright colours used in the show-ring, but he does distinguish light and dark shades. Another difference is that he judges the distance of his fences by their ground-line, and has difficulty in telling the position of a raised single pole, so it helps him to jump well if an upright fence such as a gate or wall has a low fence placed a short distance in front of it.

As a beginner you have to leave it to your pony to judge where to take off for his jump, but as you gain experience you will learn to control both his speed and his stride and to show him by your leg pressure the exact moment for taking off.

Endurance Tests, Horse Trials, Showing and Dressage

Training for endurance tests and horse trials must be slow, taking several months of good feeding and progressive exercise till maximum fitness is achieved. Then give your horse from 24 to 36 hours of complete rest, on a reduced diet, before the day.

For success in the show-ring your horse or pony must have good conformation and move well, true to type according to the class he is entered in, and he must be sound and in perfect condition. To make the most of him requires long training of yourself in riding skill and of your horse to move with brilliance and perfect control.

Dressage is the refinement, development and extension of the ordinary schooling already described. Dressage competitions take place in three main grades from elementary to advanced. This is equitation, the art of co-operation in precise movements between horse and rider, culminating in *haute ecole* or high-school riding, seen at its best in the

Spanish Riding School of Vienna. All dressage work should be practised slowly, patiently and progressively, horse and rider concentrating on their work yet relaxed and at ease, and a good teacher is essential. It is quite different from the violent horsemanship often seen in the circus ring.

Finally, whether you are training for competitions or for general improvement, remember that it does no good to let your horse get bored, and he will take more interest in his work if you give him plenty of variety. He needs recreation and enjoyment as much as you do, so after schooling take him out into the countryside to walk on a loose rein, canter on grass, jump ditches, bushes and logs for the joy of it, and go out in the company of other riders if you can, so long as they also are considerate to their horses.

Foal-handling

The way a foal is handled from the first makes all the difference to his behaviour and to his response to training later. The right way of handling is described in this book because inexperienced people sometimes buy a foal thinking that it is a cheap way of obtaining a horse or pony, and not realising that they will have to feed and care for him for four years, and then pay to have him trained before he is ready for riding. Another reason for needing to know about foals is that owners sometimes use for breeding, instead of parting with her, a much loved small pony outgrown by the children.

If you have bought an unhandled foal, perhaps from one of the free-living herds, he will be miserable and terrified at this sudden disruption of his well-adjusted natural life with his mother and other foals of the herd. He will have a desperate urge to escape to find them, for in nature if he had not this strong instinct he might not survive. But foals have another instinct also which can be made use of to help them to adapt, an intense curiosity.

For the first 48 hours after being separated from his mother it is best to put him in a securely fastened loose-box or, failing that, in a small paddock, well-fenced, not with barbed-wire. In his anxiety he will dash about wildly, becoming over-heated, exhausted and liable to chill, so a stable is much better than a paddock. See that he has water, bring him cut grass, in small quantities at a time, if he is stabled. Hay or other dry foods will probably mean nothing to him unless he can see another horse eating it. Stay near to him as long and as often as you can, just inside or just outside the stable or paddock, but do not approach him; to do this might make him kick, and you want him to learn to think of you as a friend, in place of his mother, not as an enemy. Sooner or later curiosity will make him come and sniff you, and if you keep still he will take grass from your hand. If your hand has been rubbed in sugar, he will discover that taste and will soon be glad to come to you. Before long he will let you touch him very gently at first on neck and chest, and then gradually all over, until you can put a small halter, called a foal-slip, on and off his head repeatedly without trouble.

A foal born at your home you can caress the first day, though a day or two later the mare's instinct to protect him may make her keep him from you. If this is so, let the mare come to you often to lick sugar from your hands, and the foal, who copies his mother in everything, will soon do the same, so you will be able to touch him again. If the mare is a trusting friend it is much easier, and you will be able to handle the foal daily from birth, even lifting him up, by circling your arms round his chest and hindquarters.

When your home-bred foal is about a month old, or your bought foal tame enough to feed from your hand, this is the time to teach him to lead in a halter, beginning by persuading him to lead about in his box, to and fro, round about, as you ask. Then, if you are lucky and he is home bred, while someone else leads the mare he will allow you to lead him, following her. But young foals have the instinct of all wild creatures to resist capture and the pull of the head-rope, making him walk instead of gambolling about, may drive him into a frenzy of struggling, leaping and flinging himself on the ground. So long as he is held firmly, this will happen only once, and he will quickly learn to lead quietly. Obviously it is important that this lesson should take place where the ground is soft, not in a hard-surfaced stable yard, and that the trainer should be someone with the strength to see that he cannot break away; two people may be needed.

Give him daily leading practice, at first preferably with the mare being led ahead of him, until he will walk, turn and stop as asked. Always keep level with his shoulder, never ahead of him, and if he

Six-months old foal enjoying a gallop.

Two-year old, not yet ready for training, turned out with a foal, not hers.

First lessons on the lunge-rein at 3 years old.

1. Walk on.

2. Whoa.

A four-year old pony backed by an experienced light rider.

Schooling, directed by the trainer.

Preparation for jumping. trotting over a pole.

The first jump, over a very low fence.

stops and is unwilling to move forward encourage him by voice and by tapping lightly on his flank where a rider's heel would be. Be very patient, and reward him with gentle words and with a titbit when he responds. It is most important never to try to pull him from in front, because his reaction to that is to resist strongly, pulling back and then rearing, the last thing you want to teach him.

After daily leading practice for two or three weeks, you can teach him to stand quietly when tied up. Tie him with a quick-release knot about 3 feet (1 metre) from his head to a strong fence post, or to a ring inside or outside the stable, not lower than the height of his muzzle. Stay within a few yards of him, ready to release him if he becomes upset. After a few attempts to pull free, if you soothe him he will be willing to stand quietly, and each day you can increase the length of time he is tied up and your distance from him, but do not leave him for long or go far away at this early age. Make sure that he is securely tied every time, because unless he believes from the start that escape is impossible, he will always be liable to break loose.

At this stage it is easy to teach him to move over, as described in Chapter 1, holding out your arm towards his quarters or pushing them to show him which way, and rewarding him when he stands quietly. Now you can groom him gently—a soft water-brush used dry is best— first the neck, then the back and eventually all over. If he has been handled from birth there will be no difficulty. Then teach him to have his feet lifted, also described in Chapter 1, at first lifting them for a moment only and putting them down gently. The front feet are no trouble, but patience is needed with the hind-feet, since instinct makes him react with a kicking movement.

In all his training give him constant encouragement by voice and frequent rewards when he does as you ask, and check him by a firm "No" when he resists. It is natural for foals to kick frequently and suddenly, so keep away from his heels, close to his shoulder. Every time he kicks out at you say "No", and if you can do so instantly, not otherwise, tap the offending leg sharply with a very light stick. Gradually he will learn not to kick, but do not let strange dogs or people go near his heels.

You can continue your foal's training by taking him for walks along the road, a quiet one to start with, to accustom him to traffic. If you offer him a titbit each time a car passes, that occupies his mind and he soon becomes indifferent to them. Large vans and cattle trucks are more of a difficulty, because of his instinctive fear of anything high up above him. It is a great help to traffic training if he can be kept in a roadside field before taking him out on the road and it also helps if you can let him inspect your own car, both stationary and moving slowly.

If you have a horse-box, or can borrow one, it is useful to get him to go in and out of it while he is young, so that he will have no fear when he has to travel in one.

This is all you need to teach your foal until he is three years old, and if you have always been patient and kind, yet firm, you and he will have enjoyed the training and become friends. It is all a matter of persuasion, not coercion. Titbits are invaluable for training, but a word of warning is needed. Foals are so attractive that children, and others, find it hard to resist feeding them, and this makes some foals greedy and demanding, leading to nipping at clothes or hands and even biting.

It is not necessary for the training to be continuous, without a break in time, and if during any lesson either you or he seems to be out of humour, or for any other reason, you can break off the training for days or for weeks and he will carry on from where you left off. Naturally the more you handle him and talk to him the more friendly and amenable he will become, and you will be rewarded for your patience and care in training your young foal as he develops that most valuable quality, a reliable temperament.

The cavesson for lungeing straps firmly round chin and jowl, and the rein is attached to the front of the nose-band

Well-trained horse and experienced rider competing in a national jumping championship competition.

Success in the show-ring. Diana Clapham on Tonto, British Supreme Champion Working Pony.

Making friends with a foal.

Walking a yearling.

Curiosity.

Curiosity again.

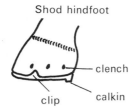

Shod hindfoot

clench

clip

calkin

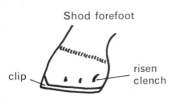

Shod forefoot

clip

risen clench

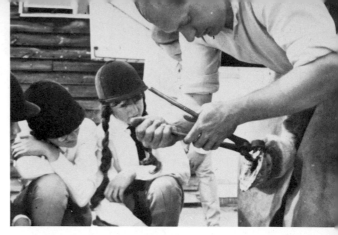

A mobile forge. *Above:* the farrier removing the old shoe ; *below:* paring the hoof into shape

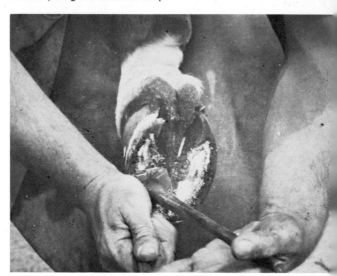

Heating the new shoe . . . and shaping it while hot

7 Health

YOUR WELL CARED FOR horse will normally be in good health and fit for the work asked of him and by correct handling you will avoid the accidents which result from carelessness. But you will need to know how to look for and recognise common ailments and injuries, how to give first aid and how to know when veterinary help is necessary.

The Feet

The need for daily attention to the feet has been stressed in Chapter 4. The spaces between the walls of the hoof and the frog must be kept clear of stable dirt and wedged stones, the hooves must not be overgrown or damaged, the shoes must be firm, no clenches risen and not worn too thin. Maintaining the feet in good condition is of the utmost importance, because neglect can cause damage which may be permanent and incurable, not just temporary lameness, and then you will understand only too well the old saying, "No foot no horse".

The horse's weight is supported on the hard edges of the walls of the hoof and on the frog, which gives both spring and grip. The walls of the hoof grow all the time, and in wild horses living in their natural habitat of dry grassland the hoof becomes hard enough not to split or chip, and growth is matched by wear. Horses and ponies kept out at grass without shoes are usually on ground too soft and damp to wear down the hoof properly or to harden it enough, though some small ponies do have very hard hooves. When the hoof grows too long, the frog no longer touches the ground and in time will shrink and become useless. The toe grows longer than the heel, altering the weight distribution on bones of the feet and tendons of the leg, and this can cause not only temporary strains but even incurable disease. Sand-crack, a vertical splitting of the hoof, if not attended to at an early stage causes permanent lameness.

The shod hoof, of course, cannot be worn away at all, and so the frog will soon lose contact with the ground and the foot its shock-

Ponies in good condition turned out after the summer holidays.

A small pony easily becomes too fat.

Soft condition: not fit for riding.

Poor condition: a pony needing food and veterinary care.

Show condition.

Hard condition: Mary Gordon-Watson on Cornishman, winner in International Horse Trials.

absorber, leading to other damage. Also the shoe becomes displaced forwards as the toe grows long, and soon the shoe rests partly on the sole instead of the wall of the foot, causing lameness through painful corns. Therefore, apart from loose shoes or risen clenches, which obviously need immediate attention, it is essential to visit the farrier or have him visit you at least once every six weeks. He will trim the walls of the feet to the correct shape and length, and if they are worn thin he will fit new shoes, but if not much worn he will replace the old ones. The farrier will use his skill and knowledge to prevent foot troubles, and when possible he will correct faults by means of special shoeing. The good farrier fits the shoe to the foot, not the foot to the shoe, and it is easier for him to make a perfect fit if he can heat the shoe at his forge or with a portable fire. Cold shoeing by untrained people is bound to lead to trouble.

If a shoe becomes loose when you are out riding—you can tell by the sound it makes on hard ground—you must walk your pony either home or to the farrier, because of the danger of the shoe swinging sideways to cut the opposite leg. If the shoe has come off, again you should walk, if possible on soft ground, and if there is none you should dismount and lead.

Soundness

As explained in Chapter 3, before buying a horse or pony you should have him tested for soundness by a veterinarian. He will examine the eyes for good vision, the legs and feet for any obvious defects, testing for lameness at the walk and trot. He will check the heart by listening to it before and after a brisk canter, and the wind—lungs and breathing—by listening for any abnormal sounds during and after exercise. He will look for any signs of skin disease, lumps or swollen glands. His certificate of soundness refers to the moment of testing, not to any faults which may develop later. Chapters 4 and 5 on feeding, exercise and shelter describe the daily care needed to keep your horse sound.

Condition

Not only every horse-owner but even people who ride occasionally would do well to learn how to judge the condition of a horse, for their own sakes as well as for the horse's. This knowledge comes from experience and observation, watching all sorts of horses and asking people who really know. It is easy to see that winners of show classes are in perfect condition with their shining coats, alert manner with bright eyes, and their smooth contours resulting from good muscles under just the right amount of fat. In lush pastures you are likely to see horses looking much fatter, with large rounded bellies, but probably lacking muscle on neck and loins. They are in soft condition, blown out with grass and not fit for hard work. On the race-course you may see horses so lean that their ribs show slightly, but you can see the muscles ripple under the skin, and this is hard condition, the best for extreme exertion, and it is achieved by carefully regulated grain feeding and daily exercise, much of it at slow paces.

Anyone can keep a horse or pony in good condition, even show condition, by feeding and exercise suited to the time of year, as described in Chapter 3. You can avoid soft condition due to too much grass and too little exercise in summer, or poor condition due to lack of good protein foods in winter. Poor condition in summer is easily recognised by spine, ribs and hip-bones standing out, which in winter may be hidden by a thick coat. So it is important to know about other signs of poor condition, such as thin necks, heads held low, dull eyes and listless manner, a staring coat, rough and dull. Movement may be slow and clumsy, in extreme cases the feet dragging and legs brushing against one another. If you find horses for hire showing any of these signs of poor condition you will know that they are either under-fed, overworked, ill (for instance with worms), much too young or much too old. Such animals need rest and special care and they are unfit for work, whatever their owners may say. They may also suffer from lameness and saddle or girth sores, since poor condition makes these troubles more likely. You will be glad of the knowledge to avoid riding schools or hiring centres which keep horses in poor condition, relying on their customers knowing no better. Ponies in trekking centres have been particularly liable to abuse, most of the riders being complete novices unable to judge condition, and by clumsiness in the saddle adding to the ponies' discomfort and fatigue.

If in spite of every care your own horse loses condition you need veterinary advice.

Above: Grazing cropped almost bare in early spring.

Right: Winter grazing of no feeding value: the yearling is fed on hay and horse-nuts.

Below: Mare and Foal: the first day.

Right and below: Flies are the enemy of foals in summer.

Right: A typical group of two mares with their foals.

Worms

Horses and ponies cannot avoid picking up the eggs of parasitic worms when grazing pastures where other horses have been. One variety, redworm, abounds where pastures are overstocked with horses, and severe infestation can be fatal in a short time if not treated. Fortunately worms can be completely controlled by giving worm powders. Your veterinarian will prescribe them for use regularly twice a year, mixed into a feed. Even foals need this protection.

Teeth

Horses of any age may occasionally suffer from toothache or a gum abscess which need immediate veterinary attention, and every horse over eighteen years old should have his teeth inspected by the veterinarian at least once a year. He will file off rough edges which develop on the grinding teeth; if not attended to, the horse gets indigestion from not being able to chew properly and he may drop lumps of half-chewed grass from his mouth.

Eyes

The corners of the eyes should be wiped when necessary with a clean damp sponge, not the same one as it used to sponge the sheath and dock. In summer the eyes need protection from flies by providing shelter, company, fly repellant (cover the eyes with your hand while applying it) and if necessary a string fringe attached to a headcollar. If flies are allowed to gather on the eye-lids they cause inflammation of the eye and sore eye-lids. You will need veterinary help to put this right, and for any eye injury or suspicion of blindness.

Ears

If a horse frequently shakes his head there may be a foreign body or an infestation of mites in the ear. The inside of the ear is very delicate and only the veterinarian should attend to it. Normally the ear is protected by a thick growth of hair inside it and this should not be trimmed away, as is often done for show purposes.

Indigestion

Out at grass indigestion usually shows in loose, sloppy droppings, due to such things as too much wet grass or too many windfall apples in an orchard. The remedy is to stable your horse or pony for part of each day with a hay-net, and of course gather up the apples frequently. When a stabled animal is turned out to grass in the spring, it is important to let him graze for only an hour or so each day at first. The digestion has to adapt to the change in diet, and ponies can be killed by turning them out in lush pasture from stable feeding or even from hay feeding on bare pasture.

Constipation is not likely in a grass-kept horse, and you would be unlikely to know about it. In the stable you should notice if droppings are few and give a warm bran mash, with Epsom salts. This is made by adding boiling water to two or three pounds of bran and one or two tablespoons of Epsom salts in a bucket; there must be only just enough water to mix with the bran and it should be given warm, not hot.

Colic

This may be due to indigestion and is sometimes caused by obstruction of the bowel, which is very serious. Signs of an attack are refusing food, uneasiness, looking round at the flank, frequently lying down and getting up again, even sitting as a dog does, and in extreme cases sweating with pain. Call the veterinarian at once and while waiting for him walk your horse about, even if it is night time. Put a rug on him unless the weather is very warm, and make sure he does not lie down, eat or drink. He may be frantic with the pain, so you will have to control him as best you can to prevent him from injuring himself. Only give a drench if so advised by the veterinarian, who may give injections to ease the pain, and he will give treatment according to the type of colic diagnosed. An acute colic may pass quickly and a less acute but longer lasting colic can be the most dangerous.

If it is a severe case you may have to stay in the stable with the horse day and night until he is better. This is to prevent him lying down, which he will want to do, but which is the cause of a twisted gut and death. Horses become more liable to colic in old age, and it can be caused at any age by a mistake in feeding. Drinking after a heavy feed of grain after a long period without food or water, eating a lot of acorns or eating frosted grass on an empty stomach are common causes; another is a pony gaining access to a grain bin and gorging himself, so make sure that gates and doors are really secure.

Poison

Symptoms similar to those of colic can result from eating poisonous plants such as rhododendron, ragwort and yew. Fortunately many horses, and particularly ponies, know to avoid poisonous plants, but it is not safe to rely on this. Poisonous hedge-clippings are especially dangerous, eaten unawares while grazing, and a horse cannot get rid of poison by vomiting, as a dog does. It is also possible for a horse to accept poisonous food offered by hand if his field adjoins a public road or right of way.

Coughs and Colds

Horses like to greet one another by blowing into each other's noses, so infections are easily spread even in the open, and much more quickly in stables. Two or three coughs at the start of exercise are normal for some horses, but anything more than this is likely to be the result of infection, and care must be taken to avoid pneumonia and permanent damage to the wind. Even if normally living out, your pony must be brought into the stable, with plenty of ventilation and a rug if necessary. Discharge should be wiped from the nose, and relief in breathing can be given by an inhalation, holding under the nose a bucket containing hay sprinkled with eucalyptus oil and boiling water. If the illness is at all severe, for instance if the temperature rises above 102°F. (36·7°C.), the veterinarian should be called, since antibiotics may be needed. The temperature is taken by gently inserting a well-greased thermometer in the rectum, holding it there for the necessary two or three minutes. The cough can be helped by applying an electuary, a sticky cough remedy, to the tongue. In convalescence exercise at the walk will be necessary for a week or more, until the cough has completely gone.

Other Illnesses

There are a number of other illnesses, most of them uncommon and some of them dangerous, so if your horse has any unusual symptoms you need veterinary advice at once.

Injuries

Tetanus is a well-known and serious disease which enters the blood stream through an injury, even a scratch. It used to be necessary to give an injection for every accidental cut or wound, but there is now a vaccine which protects for life. If you buy a horse or pony which has not a certificate to prove that he is protected, ask your veterinarian to give him the injections without delay. Death from tetanus can follow without any wound having been seen; there may perhaps have been a small injury to the sole of the foot or to muddy fetlocks.

A wound or tear of any size in the skin must be stitched by the veterinarian, who will advise on any further treatment and on exercise. Small wounds should be inspected for thorns and bathed with a dilute mild antiseptic solution (not carbolic) or with salt water, and then dusted with sulphonamide powder.

Girth Galls and Saddle Sores

If the skin is broken, these should be treated in the same way as other minor wounds. The girth or saddle must be examined for any fault, which if found must be corrected, and in any case the horse must not be saddled again until the sores are fully healed and the skin strong again. A saddle sore may take the form of a lump with the skin as yet unbroken. It may be due to an ill-fitting saddle so narrow that it pinches the shoulder, or the cantle so long as to bruise the back; the cause must be found and remedied.

Lameness

Your horse may go lame while you are out riding, and if he starts to nod his head unevenly, you must dismount. You may be able to remove the cause, for instance a stone in the foot, but if not you must lead your horse home. If the lameness is severe—hopping lame—you must send for a veterinarian, who may advise you to order a horse-box or ambulance. Trying to walk with a cracked bone or badly torn tendon could make the condition incurable. More often lameness is noticed when leading your horse out of the stable, or bringing in a pony from his field. You will want to know which is the lame leg; the best way to tell is to get someone else to lead him away from you at a walk and, if the lameness is slight, return at a trot. It is not always easy to tell, because the horse will nod his head down as an injured hind-leg touches the ground and the other way round if the trouble is in a fore-leg. You will then look for any swelling, possibly with heat, on the suspected leg, often in the fetlock due to bruising or a strained tendon.

You must never ride a lame horse, your own or a hired one, though if the trouble is slight freedom to walk about in a paddock may be better than standing in a stable getting stiff. If there is heat in a strained tendon, frequent application of cold-water bandages or hosing with cold water may help, but if the heat is due to an infected wound, for instance in the sole of the foot or on the coronet, the foot should be bathed in a bucket of hot (not too hot) water with some disinfectant in it, adding more hot water as it cools. All wounds in the foot should be seen by a veterinarian in the first instance, as what may appear to be a small wound on the surface could be an underrun sole which needs extensive cutting of the hoof. If the infection is on the leg, hot fomentations may be needed. Boiling water is poured on to a piece of lint, which is then wrung out in a cloth, tested on the back of your hand for heat and applied to the leg, quickly covering it with a piece of waterproof plastic and a thick pad of gamgee or cotton-wool which is bandaged into place. Or make a poultice by heating kaolin, spreading it between two pieces of lint, or use animalintex, again testing its heat before applying it under padding and a bandage. This should be done afresh every few hours.

If you can find no obvious and easily curable cause for the lameness you need veterinary help since there are very many possible causes, such as a strained shoulder, faulty shoeing, splints and bone disease.

Laminitis is a painful inflammation of the hoof, and as it usually occurs in all four feet, it may not show at first as lameness. The hoof may feel warm to the touch, and when the trouble has been present for some time, even if very slightly, enlarged rings appear, growing down the hoof. A common cause, particularly with ponies, is eating too much rich spring grass, and the precaution of shutting ponies in the stable for part of each day has been mentioned in Chapter 5. Severe attacks cause extreme pain and the hooves may become permanently deformed.

Skin Diseases

A well-groomed healthy horse or pony seldom has skin trouble, but one in poor condition may be found to have lice, especially in early spring, and possibly either mange or ring-worm; diagnosis by the veterinarian is essential to know what treatment is needed. Advice is needed as soon as any bare or sore patches appear, since skin troubles can spread very quickly and infect other animals, even yourself. You may have to scrub your horse all over with the warm solution prescribed, possibly more than once, and disinfect grooming tools and horse blankets.

Sweet-itch is an unsightly skin trouble, distressing to the horse and as yet incurable. It appears in summer as irritable sores on the withers and at the base of the tail, and is now thought to be an allergic condition due to grass pollen or the bite of a fly. Anyway, stabled horses are less likely to be affected than those out at grass, but once a horse has had it, he is likely to get it every summer.

Mare and Foal

An outgrown pony mare is often used for breeding, or a mare needing long rest from work because of some foot or leg trouble such as sand-crack or a splint. It is important to know how old the mare is, because, unless you have reason to know that she has previously foaled, it is wrong to breed from her for the first time after the age of fourteen years, and do not let anyone persuade you otherwise. Mares which have bred regularly can continue to the age of twenty or more. Obviously, also, a mare which is unfit for work because of some disease should not be used for breeding. Before deciding on a foal you need to be sure that you have the good grazing essential for the mare while she is carrying her foal and later while suckling it.

The stallion chosen should be about the same size as the mare, within a few inches.

The mare carries her foal for eleven months and, except that she no longer comes in season every three weeks in the summer, her condition is not apparent for the first eight months. During this time she needs light daily exercise and she can be ridden at slow paces. Feeding should of course be adequate, with plenty of hay and some horse-nuts in winter, but the food must not be too rich, especially for ponies.

During the last three months, more nourishing food is needed, which for late spring births the grass should provide, but for an early spring foal or one in late summer the mare will need extra feeding both before foaling and after. At this time cut green food, grass, clover or lucerne helps the milk supply.

Moorland ponies foal successfully in the open, but it is best at foaling time to bring your mare into the stable for shelter from cold and wet, and in case help is needed with a difficult birth. She will need a roomy loose-box, well cleaned out and deeply bedded with straw, piled up well against the walls. A field shelter would do, so long as the open side is closed with rails or hurdles to keep the mare in and other ponies out. When the birth is expected, if possible you should be at hand, and this can be difficult since births are so often at night. Usually foals are born after a few hours' labour, and the birth itself must be quick for the foal to survive. So if the birth is impeded, for instance by one of the foal's legs being out of place, veterinary help is needed urgently. Normally the mare will release the foal from the membrane and lick it dry, which stimulates it so that within half an hour it is standing up and sucking. If the mare is too weak to attend to it, you should see that its head is clear of the membrane and gently rub it dry with a towel. Offer the mare a drink of water and some green food or a bran mash. If the after-birth has not come away or the foal is not sucking within an hour, call the veterinarian.

The mare and foal should be kept in the stable for from eighteen to twenty-four hours, or longer if the weather is bad, and if the mare has lost condition give her extra dry feeds, grain or horse-nuts, for as long as necessary. Most of all she needs rich grazing, or green food cut and carried to her a little at a time so that it does not ferment before she eats it. It is usual to warn against lawn mowings, because they heat and ferment very quickly, but they are good food if given with great care in small quantities at a time; but remember not to give them until two or three mowings after the application of lawn sand or any other dressing to the lawn.

The foal will learn by copying his mother in everything, and within a few weeks will be grazing with her. At six months he should no longer be dependent on her milk, though if they are left together she may suckle him through the winter. Foals should not be bought or sold younger than six months old, except with the mare. If you have no other horses (or donkeys) and want to buy a foal, you should buy two. They need one another's company for normal development in their first year or two, and anyone who keeps one foal alone ought to devote a lot of time to it, grooming it and taking it for walks. It will want to indulge in horse-play with you, which you may be tempted to allow while it is small, but you must not, because this play soon becomes dangerous and makes future training difficult.

Even if your foals are of a breed which will eventually grow thick coats, and become ponies which live out at grass, they need to be stabled at night in their first winter. It is the time in their lives that they are growing fastest, and so they must be very well fed. They should be offered all the good quality hay they will eat, and also daily rations of about six pounds (3 kilograms) of horse-nuts, or of three pounds ($1\frac{1}{2}$ kilos) of crushed oats with three pounds ($1\frac{1}{2}$ kilos) of bran. This should be divided into two or three feeds in the day, introduced gradually in autumn, and decreased as the spring grass begins to grow. You may think that this shelter and feeding is not necessary, since moorland ponies living out in the wild are only hand-fed in very severe weather, but the herd knows where to find shelter and the foals continue to take milk from the mares; also there is no doubt that both mares and foals suffer privation and in a hard winter some of them die.

Food is so scarce in the wild that the spring grass is eaten down as soon as it grows. But the foals in your field may need to be shut in for part of each day, because too much rich grass causes laminitis, the painful inflammation of the hooves which may damage them for life.

Old Age

The life-span of horses and ponies varies from about 25 years to over 40, but from the age of sixteen most of them will not be fit for strenuous competitive work. If used with consideration they may well be fit for light work for many more years, particularly ponies, but not for the long working hours of riding establishments.

When your horse no longer has the strength for the work you want from him, you may yourself be able to pension him off for the rest he has earned. It is no kindness just to turn him out to grass by himself and forget him. He needs company, regular care for his feet and teeth,

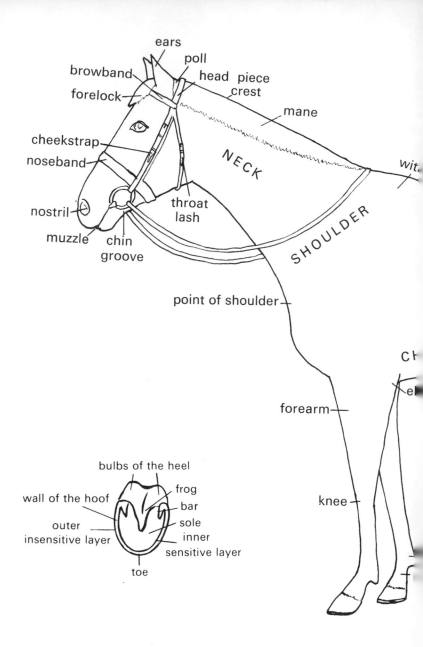

ears
poll
browband
head piece
forelock
crest
mane
cheekstrap
NECK
noseband
wit.
nostril
throat
lash
muzzle
chin
groove
SHOULDER

point of shoulder

CH

e

forearm

bulbs of the heel
frog
wall of the hoof
bar
outer
sole
insensitive layer
inner
sensitive layer
toe

knee

Points of the horse

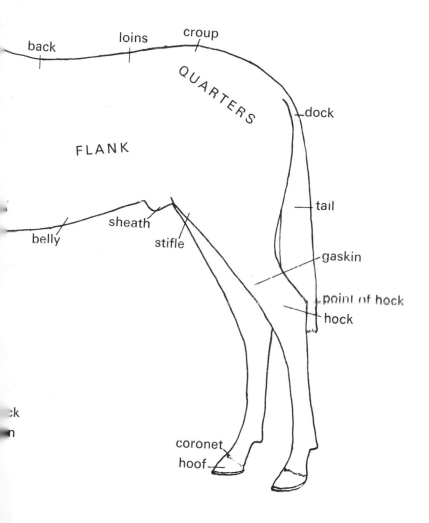

back   loins   croup

QUARTERS

FLANK

dock

tail

belly   sheath   stifle

gaskin

point of hock

hock

ːk

ɲ

coronet

hoof

shelter from heat and flies, as well as a warm, dry stable in winter. As he grows old he needs plenty of easily digested nourishing food, such as bran, grass meal and molasses. An old horse easily loses condition, often because the digestion fails, and then it is best to have him put down before he suffers a painful attack of colic. It is only fair to get the veterinarian or the horse slaughterer to shoot him with the humane killer in his own stable, and to stay with him to the last yourself; then he will have no apprehension or pain. It may be more profitable and easier for you to let the knacker take him to his own premises, but that means he is in unpleasant and strange surroundings, where he may be kept for some time before slaughter, or even sold again to work out his last days in misery. If for any reason you cannot keep your ageing horse you should not think of selling him in the open market, and if you cannot find a home for him with people who love horses and understand their needs, then it is best to see him put down.

The old pony retired but not forgotten

GLOSSARY

A

AIDS Signals by which rider directs horse.

B

BACKING (1) Horse walking backwards. (2) Horse carrying rider for first time.

BALANCED Horse moving with weight, including rider, well distributed between forehand and hindquarters.

BENDING Horse moving alternately to right and left, in and out of a line of poles.

BLANKET For extra warmth under rug of stabled horse.

BOLTING Running away out of control.

BUCKING Leaping in air with arched back.

C

CANTER Pace of three-beat rhythm.

CHILLED WATER Slightly warmed water.

CLENCH, RISEN Tip of shoe-nail pulled loose.

CLIPPED The winter coat cut short.

COLLECTED, WALK, TROT, CANTER Moving with short energetic strides.

CONDITION State of general health and nourishment.

CONFORMATION Body structure, proportions.

CORONET Line where leg joins hoof.

CRACKED HEELS Inflammation of heels, with discharge.

CRUPPER Strap from saddle with loop under tail.

D

DRENCH Liquid medicine.

DIAGONAL One foreleg and the opposite hindleg.

E

EQUITATION The art of riding.

EVENT Horse trial competition including dressage, show-jumping, speed and endurance.

EXTENDED, WALK, TROT, CANTER Opposite of collected. Long energetic strides.

F

FARRIER Expert in shoeing and care of horses' feet.

FENCE (1) Obstacle for jumping. (2) Means of enclosing a field.

FOREHAND That part of horse in front of saddle.

G

GALLOP Fast pace of four-beat rhythm.

GRAZING (1) A field of grass. (2) Eating grass in field.

H

HACKING Going for a ride.

HALTER Headpiece with noseband, of webbing.

HAY Dried flowering grass, clover, etc.

HEADCOLLAR Headpiece with noseband and throat-lash, of leather.

HEADROPE Short rope. (1) attached to halter. (2) For attaching to headcollar.

HORSE 15 hands (1·50 m.) and over. (1) Of either sex. (2) Male. (3) Stallion.

HORSEMASTERSHIP The care of horses in every respect.

HORSE-NUTS Pellets made from grain and hay.

HORSE-SICK Pasture unfit for grazing through excess droppings.

I

IMPULSION Energy derived from hindlegs.

INDOOR (OR COVERED) SCHOOL Large rectangular building for riding, with soft floor.

J

JOGGING Pace half-way between a walk and a trot.

L

LAID HEDGE Long branches of hedge cut three-quarters through and laid horizontally.

LAMINITIS Painful inflammation in the hoof.

LIGHT IN HAND Horse in perfect control with only light touch on reins.

LOOSE-BOX Enclosed compartment for one horse, in stable.

N

NUMNAH (1) Felt saddle. (2) Felt or sheepskin placed under leather saddle.

P

PACE Gait.

PONY Under 15 hands (1·50 m.).

PONY TREKKING Day-long rides at slow paces.

PONY CUBES Similar to horse-nuts.

Q

QUARTERS Hindquarters.

R

REARING Standing on the hindlegs.

REIN, ON A LOOSE Riding with the reins slack.

REIN, ON THE LEFT Circling or turning to the left.

S

SEAT Position in the saddle.

SHOWING Competing in classes judged for conformation and movement.

SHYING Sudden sideways jump.

SOUNDNESS Good health: absence of physical defects.

STALL Compartment for one horse open at one end, in stable.

STRAW Bedding made of dried stems of wheat or oats.

T

TACK Saddle, bridle, headcollar, etc.

THRUSH Infection of frog of foot.

TROT Pace in two-time rhythm.

U

UNBALANCED Opposite of balanced.

W

WELL-MANNERED Well-trained and responsive.

WIND Lungs and windpipe: breathing.

WITHERS Prominence at junction of neck and back.

SOME SOCIETIES AND CLUBS

Association of British Riding Schools. The Moat House Bungalow, Alconbury Hill, Huntingdon.
List of approved riding schools, and examination for Grooms' Diploma.
British Horse Society. National Equestrian Centre, Kenilworth, Warwickshire.
List of approved riding schools, riding clubs, and examinations for Instructors' Certificates and Horsemasters' Certificate.
The Pony Club. National Equestrian Centre, Kenilworth, Warwickshire.
Branches in twenty countries. Instructional rallies, competitions, camps.
The Ponies of Britain Club. Brookside Farm, Ascot, Berkshire.
List of approved trekking centres, pony shows.
The Royal Society for the Prevention of Cruelty to Animals. 105 Jermyn Street, London, S.W.1.
Branches throughout England and Wales.
The International Society for the Protection of Animals. 106 Jermyn Street, London, S.W.1 and 655 Boylston Street, Boston 02116, Mass., U.S.A.
Membership of 152 animal welfare societies in 56 countries.

A SHORT READING LIST

BOOKS
Horse Keepers' Encyclopedia. W. H. Walter. Elliot.
Instructions in Ponymastership. Glenda Spooner. Museum Press.
The Manual of Horsemanship. Pony Club.
Equitation. Henry Wynmalen. Country Life.

MAGAZINES
Riding.
The Light Horse.
Pony.

Index

ACKNOWLEDGEMENTS

Acknowledgements are due to the following for the use of photographs:

Australia House for "Brumbies" on page 6.

The Scottish Tourist Board for "Pony Trekking" on page 6.

The RSPCA-Diana Wyllie Filmstrip *The Care of Your Pony* for photograph by Sally Anne Thompson "Learning to Jump" on page 27.

Mrs. D. Hendry for "Foal Galloping" on page 82.

The RSPCA film *Freddy Comes to Stay* for thirty-three photographs.

Cover photograph by Barry Shapcott.

Other photographs are by the author, who thanks Mrs. A. Leaver and many other owners and riders for kind co-operation.